How The West was Won

THE
GUNFIGHTERS

How The West was Won

THE GUNFIGHTERS

BRUCE WEXLER

Skyhorse Publishing

Skyhorse Publishing books may be purchased in bulk at special
discounts for sales promotion, corporate gifts, fund-raising, or
educational purposes. Special editions can also be created to
specifications. For details, contact the Special Sales Department,
Skyhorse Publishing, 307 West 36th Street, 11th Floor, New York,
NY 10018 or info@skyhorsepublishing.com.

Skyhorse® and Skyhorse Publishing® are registered trademarks of
Skyhorse Publishing, Inc.®, a Delaware corporation.

Visit our website at www.skyhorsepublishing.com.

10 9 8 7 6 5 4 3 2 1

Library of Congress Cataloging-in-Publication Data is available on file.

Cover design by Sue Casebourne

Print ISBN: 978-1-63450-866-7

Printed in China

Contents

Introduction

Of all the wild characters of the Western frontier, the gunfighter was the most feared and flamboyant. They were not simply violent, for in a violent age, this was hardly unique. As the editor of the *Kansas City Journal* remarked in 1881, "The gentleman who has 'killed his man' is by no means a *rara avis*… He is met daily on Main Street." The gunfighters whose reputations have survived all had some defining characteristic that has kept their image alive: high morals, depravity, good looks, courage, mystery, vicious temper, sadism, marksmanship, or dandyism.

In fact the term "gunfighter" did not come into popular use until the 1870s. Bat Masterson was one of the first to popularize the word in his newspaper column, with his firsthand accounts of the luminaries of the West. But he generally preferred the term "mankiller."

The earlier terms used to describe a man who lived by his gun were either "man-killer" or "shootist" (as bad man Clay Allison described himself). They were an integral part of the West, and a direct result of the conditions there. Whereas the law governed disputes in the East, the gun was the Western arbiter of choice. Gunfighters worked on both sides of the legal divide, both as lawmen ("civilizers") and criminal outlaws. Many swapped sides when it suited them. Most were motivated by money, and were only loyal to their own interests.

The more specific idiom of "gunslinger" is thought to date from much later, first appearing in J. Gordon Edwards' Western movie *Drag Harlan*, of 1920. The word subsequently became popular in Western fiction, often appearing in the work of Zane Grey.

Gunfighters themselves came from a wide sweep of backgrounds: they ranged from men available as "guns for hire" in range wars or for specific contract killings, through to lawmen whose ultimate aim was to civilize the West.

The term "gunfighter" was also used to cover men who fought in gunfights, but these were far less frequent than might be supposed from western films and dime novels. To add to the confusion, "gunfight" itself was also a loose term. It could apply to a shoot-out or gun battle where several men were involved (like the 1881 incident at the O.K. Corral). But it could also refer to a duel fought with guns between just two men, where the participants squared off to each other in the

Above: Bat Masterson in later life, looking highly respectable.

Opposite page: Wild Bill Hickok, Texas Jack Omohundro, and Buffalo Bill Cody. A trio of great Westerners.

Above: Famous Western novelist Zane Grey (1872–1939).

Opposite page: N.C. Wyeth's graphic painting, "The Gunfight," captures the ferocious violence of a saloon showdown.

classic side-on stance. A good example of this would be Bill Hickok and Dave Tutt's classic gunfight fought in the square at Springfield, Missouri, in 1865.

"Gunslinging" was far more popular in Western movies than it ever was in real life. In countless Western movies, the "gunslinger" twirls his pistols around, does trick sharp shooting, and generally shows off his prowess with his weapons. This almost never happened in real life. Once drawn, it was imperative to discharge your gun as soon as possible, to avoid being shot to death. Gunslinging would have been a highly dangerous diversion from the main business of the gunfighter – staying alive.

In real life, gunmen almost never squared off to each other in the shootouts that are so popular in Western films and literature. Gunfighters had far too much respect for each other's skills to risk it, knowing that a real gunfight would be fatal for at least one of the duelists, if not both.

Indeed, well-known gunfighters were held in such general fear that they were very rarely challenged by anyone who knew their reputations. Equally, gunfighters on the wrong side of the law feared the best of the gunmen law enforcers, and sought to avoid them at all costs. (Early Western townsfolk were fully aware of this and were willing to pay large sums to high-profile gunmen to protect them, and establish law and order.) First-rate gunfighters who died violently were mostly ambushed and killed by second-rate gunmen who were far too afraid to face them openly. Several famous gunfighters were killed in this underhand way, having fallen victim to their own fearsome reputations. These fatalities included Billy the Kid, John Wesley Hardin, and Wild Bill Hickok. Others, like Jesse James, were betrayed and murdered by their own treacherous followers, caught off-guard for a few fatal moments.

In fact, reputation was often a tool of the gunfighter's trade, and he would groom it like he would hone his shooting skills. Many men of the type quite deliberately exaggerated their kill tally, including Wyatt Earp and Wild Bill Hickok. Earp was reputed to have been involved in over a hundred gunfights, but only five of these can be confirmed. Hickok's fearsome reputation netted him $150 a month to keep the peace in Abilene, but his actual kill rate was quite modest.

Despite appearances, the avowed intention of most gunfighters was to live long, and die in their beds. Some who were lucky enough to achieve this include Wyatt Earp and Luke Short. Others, like Bat Masterson, moved into other, less risky professions, and successfully outlived the violent era of the western gunfighter.

Robert Clay Allison, 'The Shootist'

Below: Robert Clay Allison is twenty-six in the conventional studio portrait.

Robert Clay Allison was no gentleman gunfighter. Clay was a moody and vicious man who bred fear in everyone who knew him. He was born on September 2, 1840, in Tennessee, the fourth of nine children born to his parents, Jeremiah Scotland Allison and Mariah R. Allison. He was born disfigured with a club foot. His father was a Presbyterian minister who made his living in the sheep and cattle business. Sadly, Jeremiah died when Clay was just five. Clay worked on the family farm at Waynesboro, Tennessee, until the age of twenty-one, but always had a reputation for having a vile temper and terrible mood swings.

On October 15, 1861, Clay joined the Tennessee Light Artillery Division of the Confederate Army. But on January 15, 1862, he was medically discharged due to "personality problems." His discharge papers described him as "incapable of performing the duties of a soldier because of a blow received many years ago. Emotional of physical excitement produces paroxysmals [sic.] of a mixed character, partly epileptic and partly maniacal." His brother Monroe was reported as a deserter in the same year. Despite his mental health problems, Clay rejoined the Confederate army in September 1862, as part of the 9th Tennessee Cavalry, serving under the famous rebel General Nathan Bedford Forrest. On May 4, 1865, Clay's company surrendered at Gainesville, Alabama. He was held as a prisoner of war for a few days, convicted of spying and sentenced to be shot. The night before his execution was scheduled, he killed his guard and made his escape. The Civil War had bred feelings of hatred for black people in Allison, and upon leaving the army he joined the embryonic Ku Klux Klan. Trudging back to the family farm, Clay encountered a Union officer who was trying to seize the property; legend has it that Clay snatched a gun from the house and shot the officer dead. Forced to keep out of view, Clay worked as a cattle hand after leaving the army, and moved to the Texan Brazos River Territory in 1865. He was accompanied by his brothers Monroe and John, his sister Mary, and her future husband, Lewis Coleman.

During this time, Clay worked as a ranch hand and trail boss, driving cattle to New Mexico. He may have been among the eighteen herders who blazed the Goodnight-Loving Trail in 1866. Things obviously went well for him, as by 1870 he had acquired his own ranch in Colfax County, New Mexico. But local newspapers were already reporting that he had dispatched as many as fifteen

Above: In this far more famous photograph, Allison is shown with his leg in plaster, having discharged his own gun into his foot.

local men, and he had a grim reputation for violence, especially when he was drunk. His first truly notorious – and grotesque – killing happened in late 1870. Allison was drinking in a saloon when a hysterical woman approached him. She told him that her husband had gone mad and killed a number of his own ranch hands at their cabin, along with their infant daughter. Allison rounded up a posse, but they found no bodies at the ranch. However, a few days later, bones were discovered on the property, and the ranch owner was arrested and imprisoned. Enraged by the man's behavior, Allison broke him out of jail, lynched him, and cut off his head, riding twenty-nine miles to Cimarron with this gruesome trophy on a pole before displaying it in a local saloon. This kind of behavior did nothing to endear people to Allison, who was clearly mad. In the spring of 1871, a prank he was involved in seriously backfired. Famously, Allison shot himself in the foot while encouraging General Gordon Granger's army mules to stampede. A famous photograph of Clay was taken at this time, complete with bandaged foot and crutch.

Allison's presence in New Mexico also attracted other killers to the area, who wanted to enhance their own reputations by adding him to their list of kills. In 1874, Chunk Colbért, for one, coolly invited Allison out to dinner before trying to shoot him under the table. Many years before, on his way across the Brazos River, Allison had severely beaten the ferryman, who happened to be Colbert's uncle, accusing

Above: A classic Bowie knife, complete with an eight-inch blade and "clip" point.

the man of cheating him. Unfortunately, Allison beat Colbert to the draw, and killed his dining companion just as coffee was served. When he was asked why he had accepted a dinner invitation from a man he knew wanted to kill him, Allison responded that he "didn't want to send a man to hell on an empty stomach."

In October of the following year (1875) Clay lynched Mexican Cruz Vega from a telegraph pole, seemingly for being involved in the killing of a Methodist circuit rider. When Vega's friend Pancho Griego attempted to revenge him, Clay shot him dead in the St. James Hotel in Cimarron. In December 1876, Clay and his brother John became involved in a saloon brawl in Las Animas, Colorado, and ended up shooting and killing the local sheriff, Charles Faber. Allison was charged for the crime, but acquitted on grounds of self-defense.

In 1876 Allison is reputed to have been involved in the murder of three black soldiers, but was never held accountable for these murders either.

In 1877, Allison had a brush with a gunman of a completely different caliber than himself: Wyatt Earp, in Dodge City, Kansas. Clay was angry about the way that cowboys were treated in the notorious town. But the two posturing gunfighters kept their fight verbal, and went on their way intact.

As time went on, Clay's behavior became increasingly deranged. He was a heavy drinker, and this must have exacerbated his problems. When a dental appointment to cure a raging toothache went awry and the nervous dentist began to drill the wrong tooth, Allison furiously bundled the dentist into his own chair and ripped off half the man's lip in trying to extract one of the dentist's own teeth.

Another event that demonstrates Allison's bizarre view of the world was the so-called Bowie knife grave affair. He had fallen into a water dispute with a neighboring rancher, and suggested that they should settle their differences by digging a grave big enough to hold them both. They should then climb into the pit, each armed only with a Bowie knife, and see which one of them survived to climb out. The victor would arrange a tombstone for the vanquished. Given the bizarre violence Allison displayed, it is very surprising that he never spent a day in jail. In the end events overtook him, and the "grave" encounter never took place.

In 1878 Allison sold his New Mexico ranch to his brother John for $700, and moved to Hemphill County, Texas, with the rest of his family. He was planning to ranch, and registered a brand for his cattle.

On February 15, 1881, Clay married Dora McCullough in Mobeetie, Wheeler County, Texas. The couple were to have two daughters. Despite his reputation, Allison served as a juror in Mobeetie, although he was also reputed to have ridden naked and drunk along the main street there. Locally, he was known as the "Wolf of the Washita."

In 1883 Allison bought a ranch in Pecos, Texas, and became involved in local politics. For some years he seemed to lead a fairly regular life, but this was cut short by an unfortunate accident. Driving supplies from Pecos back to his ranch, Allison was thrown from his wagon. One of the rear wheels of the heavily-loaded wagon ran over his neck, killing him instantly. It was July 1887, and Allison was forty-seven years of age. The following day he was buried at Pecos Cemetery. His gun was inscribed, "Gentleman gun fighter." A second marker was added sometime later with the highly unlikely description, "He never killed a man that did not need killing."

Clay's ignominious end was highly unusual for a "shootist" at this time. (Clay himself had coined this term to describe a man who lived by the gun.) Men of Allison's vicious and violent type generally expired in a hail of bullets or dancing at the end of a rope.

Billy the Kid

Below: Full-length portrait of Billy the Kid. For many years, he was thought to be left-handed because the photograph had been mistakenly reversed.

Billy the Kid, the teenage outlaw, was one of the most colorful figures and gunmen of the Old West. He was a controversial figure in both life and death. He is considered by some observers to be a cold-blooded, psychopathic killer, while others see him as a boy who "loved his mother devotedly" and was led to a life of criminality by neglectful adults. Either way, he is credited with at least six killings, and his ballad boasts that "he'd a notch on his pistol for twenty-one men."

Billy was born to Irish parents in New York City in November 1859. His birth name was William Henry McCarty Jr., but he was called Henry by his mother, Catherine. His father died when he and his brother, Joseph, were very young, and his mother died in 1874, just a year after remarrying. By this time, Billy's family was living in Silver City, New Mexico, where they had gone to seek a cure for their mother's tuberculosis. Billy's stepfather didn't want the two boys, so he put them into foster homes where The Kid, who was now fourteen, washed dishes to earn his keep. Billy's juvenile life of crime started at this time. He stole some cheese from a rancher, and was then found to be in possession of stolen clothing and firearms. Unfortunately, being locked up for this minor misdemeanor scared him so much that he decided to escape by climbing the chimney. For the next couple of years, he tramped around working as a ranch hand and gambler, trying to avoid brushes with the law. But everything went downhill rapidly after he shot and killed a bully who was teasing him. Unable to get honest work, he reluctantly joined a gang of rustlers known as The Boys. These were led by the Scotsman John R. Mackie. In 1877 an altercation with a bullying blacksmith, Frank Cahill resulted in Cahill being shot to death. Billy fled to the Arizona territory and joined the Evans Gang, a band of cattle rustlers. The gang reputedly stole animals belonging to cattle magnate John Chisum. It was during this period that McCarty was attacked by Apaches, who stole his horse and left him to wander alone in the desert. He painfully made his way to the nearest settlement, which was owned by the Jones family. They took him, and "The Kid" decided to try legitimate work, assuming a new name: William H. Bonney. He was soon working for the English rancher John Tunstall. Turnstall and Billy developed a close relationship, and many believe that Billy looked upon his employer as the father he had never had. Unfortunately, Tunstall was murdered by members of the Murphy-Dolan gang in the Lincoln County War. Knowing Tunstall's affection for his horses, the gang then shot his favorite horse and put his

Above: Tintype photograph of Billy the Kid.

hat on the dead animal's head. Distraught, Bonney joined the feud on the side of the regulators. When Lew Wallace became the governor of New Mexico in 1878, Bonney wrote to him asking for immunity in return for his testimony against Tunstall's killers. He met up with the governor, armed with a pistol and a Winchester rifle. Despite helping Wallace to convict the notorious John Dolan, Billy was kept a prisoner and was forced to make his own escape.

By now Bonney was a celebrity, and the newspapers coined the sobriquet "Billy the Kid" because of his smooth skin and youthful looks. The Kid was reputedly fed up with having every murder in the West attributed to him, and moaned that "I don't know as anyone would believe anything good of me." He managed to avoid capture for two years, but when he was framed for the murder of Deputy James Carlyle, Pat Garrett was charged with bringing him to justice. Garrett finally caught up with The Kid on December 23, 1880, in a cabin in Stinking Springs. After a brief standoff, Billy surrendered. He was charged and sentenced for the murder of Sheriff Brady during the Lincoln County War, and was taken back to Lincoln to await hanging. The Kid was fully aware that there could now be no reprieve, so he made his final escape, killing guard J.W. Bell. He also took time out to gun down Robert Olinger with his own weapon. Olinger had teased him during his prison stay. Later, The Kid said that he wouldn't have shot Bell if he hadn't tried to run away, but he offered no apology for Olinger's dispatch.

Public opinion now swung against Billy, and Pat Garrett was charged once again with bringing him to justice. It took him three months to catch up with Billy in Fort Sumter. At the very moment that Garrett was pumping rooming house owner Pete Maxwell for intelligence about the Kid's movements, Billy walked in to get a steak for dinner. Garrett felled the youngster with two bullets from his .45 caliber single-action Colt, one of which lodged in Billy's heart. The Kid spoke fluent Spanish, and his rather pathetic final words were, "*Quien es? Quien es?*" - "Who is it? Who is it?"

> *Fair Mexican maidens play guitarsand sing*
> *A song about Billy, their boy bandit king*

Billy's brief but colorful career as a gunman and outlaw was over. He was reputed to have gambled with Doc Holliday, dined with Jesse James, and shot targets with Bat Masterson.

His advice to those that would follow in his footsteps was simple: "Advise persons never to engage in killing." Many of his friends and acquaintances mourned

Opposite page: This damaged photograph portrays the tall Bob Ollinger, shot by Billy the Kid in 1881. Ruthless businessman James Dolan is seated.

Above: Pat Garrett, who hunted Billy the Kid with John W. Poe and James Brent.

his passing very sincerely, praising his sense of humor, his loyalty to his friends, his extreme bravery, and the kindness he showed to his horses. Billy looks a little simple in his portrait, but contemporaries spoke of his intelligence and cunning. Many also spoke derisively of Pat Garrett's self-interest. Garrett gained the office of sheriff of Lincoln County for his work in killing The Kid, and wrote the best-selling biography, *The Authentic Life of Billy the Kid: The Noted Desperado of the Southwest.*

But Billy was no "good bad man." By the time of his death, he was pretty well bad through and through, and many believed he was a cold-hearted murderer. But the teenage outlaw of the Southwest has left probably the biggest legend of any gun-slinging wrongdoer of the West.

I'll sing you a true song of Billy the Kid
I'll sing of the desperate deeds that he did
Way out in New Mexico long, long ago
When a man's only chance was
his own forty-four.

When Billy the Kid was a very young lad
In the old Silver City he went to the bad
Way out in the West with a gun in his hand
At the age of twelve years he first killed his man

Now this is how Billy the Kid met his fate
The bright moon was shining,
the hour was late
Shot down by Pat Garrett,
who once was his friend,
The young outlaw's life had now
come to its end.

Left: Pete Maxwell's house. It was here during the night of July 14, 1881 that Pat Garrett sat in Pete's bedroom and shot the Kid.

Colt Lightning

Above: The Colt Lightning with the standard barrel length of 4½ inches and the ejector rod.

This was the first Colt model to feature the distinctive bird's head-shaped grip that was thought to have been influenced by the Webley Bulldog , a popular English revolver of the frontier period.

Henry McCarty, alias Antrim, alias William H. Bonney, but better known to us as Billy the Kid, was in and out of scrapes for all of his short life. Starting in the Lincoln County Wars, he was credited with killing twenty-one men, one for each year of his life. His actual total was thought to be nearer to six.

In his line of work, a rapid-fire revolver would have been a valuable asset, and the aptly named Colt Lightning is on record as being Billy's favorite weapon, in .38 inch caliber. Indeed, there was strong demand for a double-action weapon, and the early models of 1877 strongly resembled the Colt Single-Action or Peacemaker on which they were based. Double action was achieved by adding a strut, which connected the trigger movement to the hammer. This allowed the trigger to slip past the strut at the top of the cycle, thus releasing the hammer. It could also be cocked manually and fired like a single-action. This did have its disadvantages. The trigger pull was necessarily stronger and there were more parts to wear out. But this did not seem to deter Billy, or indeed any of the other 165,999 purchasers of the gun. It was a popular weapon in the final years of the frontier.

SPECIFICATIONS

Caliber: 0.38

Length of barrel: 2½, 3½, and 4½ inches

Barrel shape: Round

Finish: gray with traces of original blue

Grips: Hard Rubber

Action: Double

Year of manufacture: 1877-1909

Manufacturer: Samuel Colt, Hartford, Connecticut

Above: Above: The Storekeeper version of the Lightning had no ejector rod. Instead, the arbor spindle had a knobbed end to enable it to be easily unscrewed to allow the cylinder to be removed for reloading. This one has the 2½ inch barrel.

Black Bart

Above: An early tintype of Black Bart, one of the most notorious goldfield robbers. His respectable appearance belies his true profession.

Opposite page: Gold mining was extremely labor- intensive, and only one miner in ten made any money from the goldfields.

Charles E. Bowles, Boles, or Bolton – AKA Black Bart, T.Z. Spalding, and Po8 – was one of the most notorious highwaymen of the post-Gold Rush era. He was a gentleman thief who dressed like a dandy and left doggerel poems at the scenes of his crimes. His strange sense of humor and polite manners made a strange contrast to his prolific thieving. Wells Fargo & Co. was to become Bowles's chief victim, and his nemesis.

Bowles was born in Norfolk, England, in 1829. His parents were John and Maria Bowles, who went on to have ten children. The family immigrated to the United States when Charley was two and settled on a hundred-acre farmstead in Jefferson County, in upstate New York. Strong and fit, Charley was lucky enough to survive a bout of infantile smallpox, usually fatal at the time.

In 1849, he and his brother David set up to make their fortunes in the western goldfields. After a tough winter in Missouri, the pair moved on to Sacramento, California, in 1850. But despite several attempts to strike it lucky in the Gold Rush, which resulted in the deaths of both his brothers from camp diseases, Charley was left pretty much empty-handed. In 1854 Bowles found himself back in Illinois, and married a woman named May Elizabeth Johnson. They had four children together. But Charley never liked ordinary farm life, and was quick to volunteer for the Union Army when the Civil War broke out. He enlisted with the 116th Regiment of the Illinois Infantry on August 13, 1862. He was quickly promoted to First Sergeant in Company B. During his time in the army, he took part in several major actions, including Sherman's Yazoo Expedition (December 1862 to January 1863), the assault on Fort Hindman, the siege of Vicksburg, and the Battle of Resaca. In 1864 he was severely wounded in the side and was extremely lucky to survive his injury. Despite this setback, he returned to his unit, fought in the Battle of Atlanta (featured in *Gone with the Wind*), and took part in Sherman's March to the Sea and his Campaign of the Carolinas. He finally left his regiment in June 1865. But Bowles

found life on the family farm in New Oregon, Iowa, completely stultifying and he was soon back in the goldfields. His failure there – and the reasons for it – were to have a great and malignant influence on his future. Charley had started to work a small Montana gold mine by himself using a process of running water through a series of troughs. Agents of Wells Fargo approached Charley to buy the mine, but he refused, so they cut off his water supply and ended his venture. Forced to abandon his dig, Bowles wrote to his wife about the injustice of the situation, threatening to "take steps." He wrote a final letter to Mary from Silver Bow, Montana, on August 25, 1871. Continuing his tramp around the gold regions, he lost contact with his family, and they assumed that he had died in the Western wilds.

But for eight years, between 1875 and 1883, a well-dressed and polite highwayman committed twenty-eight robberies on Wells Fargo stagecoaches across the Gold Country and California. Wearing a flour sack as a mask and garnished with a jaunty derby hat, "Black Bart," as Bowles styled himself, never fired the shotgun he carried and – terrified of horses – committed his crimes on foot. This trail of lawlessness began on July 26, 1875, when Bowles robbed the Wells Fargo Sonora-to-Milton stagecoach. He politely addressed the stage driver, John Shine, asking him to "please throw down your treasure box, sir?" His poetic signature first came to light after his 1877 robbery of the Sonoma County Point Arena-to-Duncan's Mill stagecoach. A poem, written on a waybill, was left on a tree stump under a stone:

> *I've labored long and hard for bread*
> *For honor and for riches*
> *But on my corns too long you've tred*
> *You fine-haired sons of bitches*
> *Black Bart*
> *The Po8*
> *Driver, give my respects to our friend, the other driver;*
> *But I really had a notion to hang my old disguise hat on his weather eye.*
> *Respectfully, B.B.*

On July 25, 1878, "B.B." left another poem after stealing a $200 diamond ring and $379 in cash:

> *Here I lay me down to sleep*
> *To wait the coming morrow*
> *Perhaps success, perhaps defeat*
> *And everlasting Sorrow*

Let come what will I'll try it on
My condition can't be worse
And if theres money in that box
Tis munny in my purse

Black Bart
The Po8

Over the course of his career, Charley often chatted politely with his victims. "No, don't get out," he said to a woman passenger while robbing the La Porte-to-Oroville stage in 1878. "I never bother the passengers." In 1879, he quipped to the driver of the same stage, "Sure hope you have a lot of gold in that strongbox, I'm nearly out of money." In 1881 the driver of the Yreka-to-Redding coach asked him, "How much did you make?" "Not very much for the chances I take," Bart answered. In fact, he had been stealing around $6,000 a year and living a fairly luxurious lifestyle. He preserved this modus operandi for twenty-eight holdups, most of which took place in Southern Oregon and California.

His luck finally ran out in November 1883, when he attempted to rob the Sonora-to-Milton stagecoach. Bart was shot by Jimmy Rolleri, a young man who was riding shotgun for the driver, Reason E. McConnell. Having jumped down from the driver's box to look for game, he returned to see Bart trying to hatchet open the strongbox. Jimmy managed to wing Black Bart, and even though he managed to escape with the stolen gold, he left his derby and equipment behind a nearby rock. These things proved to be his undoing. The Calaveras County sheriff found a woman who had sold Bart his provisions, but the clue that located this gentleman bandit was a laundry mark on the handkerchief he had dropped at the scene of the crime. This led Wells Fargo detective agents James Hume and Henry Nicholson Morse to his door, at 37 2nd Street, San Francisco, where he was living as Charles E. Bolton, a respectable mine

Above: Black Bart in old age. He asserted that he "never robbed a passenger, or ill-treated a human being."

engineer. Hume described him as "a person of great endurance. Exhibited genuine wit under most trying circumstances. Extremely proper and polite in behavior, eschews profanity."

Convicted of a selection of hold-ups, partly because he openly confessed to crimes perpetrated before 1879 (believing the statute of limitations had expired on these), Bart was convicted to a six-year prison sentence in San Quentin. But in 1888 he was released for good behavior after serving just four years. His health and eyesight had been affected by his time in prison, but he declined to return to his family, though he struck up a correspondence with his wife, Mary. He told her that he was sick of being shadowed by Wells Fargo, but finally gave Agent Hume the slip in February 1888.

In November that same year, a stagecoach was robbed by a masked highwayman who left a poem behind:

> *So here I've stood while wind and rain*
> *Have set the trees a-sobbin,*
> *And risked my life for that damned box*
> *That wasn't worth the robbin'.*

Hume declared that the holdup had been a copycat crime, and there are no further confirmed sightings of Charley Bowles. Rumors persisted that he had been killed at an unsuccessful hold-up, or moved to New York, Montana, or Nevada. Some people even assumed that Wells Fargo had paid Black Bart off. Whatever the truth, this gentleman of the road somehow managed to disappear like the dust on the trails he had haunted during his illustrious career.

Butch Cassidy

"As technology thrusts us relentlessly into the future, I find myself, perversely, more interested in the past. We seem to have lost something – something vital, something of individuality and passion. That may be why we tend to view the Western outlaw, rightly or not, as a romantic figure."

– Robert Redford

"The best way to hurt them is through their pocket book. They will holler louder than if you cut off both legs. I steal their money just to hear them holler. Then I pass it out among those who really need it."

– Butch Cassidy

Of all the Western gunmen and outlaws, none were more fondly remembered and celebrated in folklore than Butch Cassidy. Leader of the Wild Bunch Gang, Cassidy was known as the Robin Hood of the West. Of all the Western bandits, he and his Wild Bunch had the longest and most lucrative criminal careers. Later on, Butch

Below: An early view of Salt Lake City, complete with wagons.

Right: Robert Leroy
Parker, alias Butch
Cassidy, photographed
in the Wyoming
Penitentiary. Despite his
reputation, Cassidy was
not a killer.

and his partner, the Sundance Kid, were to continue with this successful formula, right into the twentieth century. If rumor is to be believed, he was also one of the few Western gunmen to survive into old age.

Butch was born in Beaver, Utah, on April 15, 1866. His real name was Robert LeRoy Parker. His parents were Mormons. Butch's grandfather, Robert Parker, was one of the original Mormon pioneers who set out on the long trek west to Salt Lake City. Unfortunately, he froze to death one night and was buried along the trail by his wife and oldest son, Butch's father, Maximillian. The surviving Parkers continued on to Salt Lake City and established the family in the West. As an adult, Maxi Parker helped other Mormons make their way to Utah and married Ann Campbell Gillies. The couple bought a ranch near Circleville, Utah, and raised their family there. Butch was the eldest of their thirteen children. Despite this ultra-respectable family background, once the young Butch left home, he soon fell under the influence of a local horse thief and cattle rustler, Mike Cassidy. Butch followed the venerable Western tradition of pursuing ranch work. While working at the Eugene Amaretti ranch in Wind River, Wyoming, he was described as a "crack shot, and the best there with a rope. He could ride around a tree at full speed and empty a six-gun into the tree, putting every shot within a three-inch circle." Cassidy also had a brief stint as a butcher in Otto Schnauber's Meat Market at Rock Springs, Wyoming, and this is where he acquired the sobriquet of "Butch." He adopted Cassidy as his last name in veneration of his first criminal mentor. Effectively, he had reinvented himself. In his new identity, Butch seemed free to adopt a completely different way of life than that of his parents. His first offence was trivial, shoplifting some jeans and a pie from a closed shop. At least he had the decency to leave an IOU. But although he was acquitted of this misdemeanor, it seems as though Butch continued to lead a life on the edge of criminality, trading stolen horses and rustling cattle. In 1887, Cassidy met Matthew Warner. Originally, the relationship seemed legitimate. Warner owned a racehorse, which the pair raced in Telluride and in Brown's Park on the Utah-Colorado border. They were highly successful, and divided the winnings between them. But in June 1889, Cassidy, Warner, and two associates robbed the San Miguel bank in Telluride, Colorado.

The raid netted the gang $21,000. They succeeded thanks to excellent forward planning, casing the joint thoroughly in advance of the robbery. Butch used his share of the spoils to buy a ranch near Dubois, Wyoming, and tried to make a living there. Unfortunately, he failed, and returned to his previous career of horse stealing. Cassidy was also suspected of being involved in a protection racket. Butch was

Above: The Wild Bunch. Butch Cassidy is the smiling figure at the right, Sundance is on the left.

arrested in Lander, Wyoming, and on July 15, 1894, he was sentenced to two years hard labor in the Wyoming penitentiary. His prison description portrays him as being five feet nine inches tall, with a light complexion, dark hair, and blue eyes. He was noted to be unmarried, of unknown parentage, no religion, and intemperate habits. Butch had certainly moved a very long way from his Mormon background. Released early by Governor William Alford Richards, Cassidy promised that he would not commit any further offenses in Wyoming. The "gentleman outlaw" was as good as his word, pursuing his criminal career in other states for the majority of his career. It was not until 1900 that he robbed a Union Pacific train near Tipton, Wyoming.

Over the following five years, Butch Cassidy put together a gang of skilled outlaws and masterminded a series of highly successful bank and train robberies in Idaho, Utah, New Mexico, Nevada, Texas, and Montana. Cassidy was one of the first criminals to use the so-called Outlaw Trail, a meandering path that began in Mexico, ran through Utah, and ended in Montana. The trail linked a series of hideouts and ranches that were sympathetic to outlaw cowboys.

By 1896, the gang was well-known throughout the west as the Wild Bunch and had netted over $270,000 in spoils. Cassidy himself was known as The King of the Wild Bunch. The gang included such criminal luminaries as Harry Longabaugh (the Sundance Kid, originally from Pennsylvania), Harvey Logan (Kid Curry), Bill Carver, Ben Kilpatrick (the Tall Texan), Harry Tracy, Henry Wilbur Meeks (another Mormon from Utah), and Butch's closest friend, Elzy Lay. Butch described the "Bunch" in this way to his family "There were a lot of good friends, but Elzy Lay was the best, always dependable and level-headed. Sundance and I got along fine, but he liked his liquor too much and was too quick on the trigger."

The gang was responsible for the most lucrative series of crimes in the history of the Old West, but was not considered particularly violent. It was even celebrated for fighting for settlers' rights "against the old time cattle baron." But in fact, several gang members were guilty of a number of murders, including those of Sheriff Joe Hazen, Sheriff Edward Farr, and posse man Henry Love. Ironically, it was Elzy Lay who was convicted of the murders of Farr and Love, and was sentenced to life imprisonment in the New Mexico State Penitentiary. Butch himself swore to his father that he had never killed a man, but added that "some of my boys had itchy fingers. I tried to control 'em." The gang was also famous for its wry humor. In 1901, the Wild Bunch sat for a group portrait photograph. In the resulting image, known as the Fort Worth Five photograph, the men look uncannily like the Dodge City Peace Commission with their smart suits, derby hats, and watch chains. The Pinkerton Detective Agency obtained a copy of the photograph, and used it on their wanted posters for the gang.

As railroads crossed the West and communications got better, it got harder and harder for criminals to escape the burgeoning law machine. In 1900, several Wild Bunch members were involved in shootouts with various lawmen, and Kid Curry's brothers George and Lonny were killed.

Butch and Sundance realized that their days as Western gunmen were over. Their carefully-planned strategy of using secret hideouts was becoming less and less secure. They could feel the tightening of the net as state law officials and the

Above: Formal portrait of Sundance and Etta Place, taken at De Young's studio in New York.

Pinks closed in on them. The Wild Bunch disbanded, and the pair fled east to New York City in 1901, accompanied by Sundance's girlfriend, Etta Place. From there, they set sail for Buenos Aires on the British steamship *Herminius*. Butch and Sundance bought a huge fifteen-thousand-acre ranch in Cholilo, Chubut Province, Argentina, complete with a four-room log cabin. They stocked it with thirteen hundred sheep, five hundred cattle, and thirty-five horses. But after three years of trying to live honestly, the pair became short of money again and started a campaign of robbing Argentinean banks of money and gold. They escaped with a substantial sum of money and sold the Cholila ranch. They then caught the steamship *Condor* into Chile, but were to make a further foray back into Argentina in December 1905, robbing the Banco de la Nacion in Villa Mercedes of 12,000 pesos.

In 1906 the trio split when Etta Place decided she wanted to return to America. Despite the risk, Sundance escorted her back to San Francisco. Butch got work guarding the company payroll at the Concordia Tin Mine in Bolivia, and Sundance joined him on his return. But the pair was irrevocably drawn to the easy life, and in 1908 they attacked a silver mine courier near San Vicente, Bolivia, and stole 15,000 pesos from him. A pair of bandits was subsequently tracked to a small lodging house in the town, which was soon surrounded by a posse of armed lawmen, soldiers, and the local mayor. When the Bolivians opened fire, the bandit pair returned it. A hellish fire fight opened up, and the bandits expired in a hail of

bullets. It was speculated that one of them had fatally shot his partner in crime in the head, to put him out of his misery. It was assumed that the dead men were Butch and Sundance, and the pair did nothing to disabuse this assumption.

In her 1975 book, *Butch Cassidy, My Brother*, Lula Parker Betenson claimed that her brother Butch Cassidy returned to the United States in 1908, using the alias William Thadeus Phillips. Phillips settled in Morenci, Michigan, where he married Gertrude Livesay. They then moved to Arizona. They adopted their son William Richard Phillips in 1919. According to Betenson, her brother unsuccessfully tried gold mining in Alaska before establishing the Phillips Manufacturing Company in Spokane, Washington, in 1912. He sold adding machines, farm machinery parts, automatic garage-door openers, and automobile gas mileage indicators. Lula says that in 1925, Butch attended a family reunion in Circleville, Utah, which was attended by their father Maxi, their brother Mark, and Lula herself. She maintained that Butch had told their father that he had tried to quit his life of crime on many occasions, but explained that "when a man gets down, they won't let him get up. He never quits paying his price."

In 1930 William Phillips's business failed in the depression, and Lula's book tells how Butch tried in vain to locate caches of money he had hidden during his bandit career. In 1934, he wrote his own life story, *The Bandit Invincible, the Story of Butch Cassidy*, but failed to find a publisher. Phillips died of cancer on July 20, 1937, at the age of seventy-one. He was cremated, and his ashes were scattered over the Little Spokane River.

Above: Pinkerton agents acted as Union spies during the Civil War and helped to break up the unions. The term "private eye" was inspired by their symbol.

Colt Dragoon

Below: Detail of the Cylinder showing the honest patina of age. Originally, many of these weapons had intricate engravings of combat scenes on the cylinders.

In the late 1840s, Texas became the focus of weapons activity on the Western frontier. The Alamo massacre of 1836, and the subsequent wWar of Texan Independence, resulted in a heavy demand for advanced weapons with which to defend the newly established republic. Demand for Colts was stimulated by the notable success of the Texas Paterson Colt revolvers at Hays's Big Fight. Captain Jack Hays and a detachment of fifteen Texas Rangers defeated over eighty Comanche using the weapon. The Indians had rushed the small force of Texans after their first volley of

SPECIFICATIONS

Caliber: 0.44

Length of barrel: 8 inches

Barrel shape: Round

Finish: Gray with traces of blue

Grips: Walnut

Action: Single action 6 shot repeating revolver

Year of manufacture: 1848

Manufacturer: Samuel Colt, New York City

The Colt Dragoon is one of the first models in what is regarded as the classic Colt shape. Its massive proportions and heavy brass fittings gave it an unfortunate handicap in the weight department.

shots, thinking that the Rangers had paused to reload. But the repeating handguns continued to fire, with devastating effect.

When the war with Mexico began, The Rangers were enlisted into the U.S. Cavalry and became Dragoons. This honorable name was given to the new Colt pistol, patented in 1848. The Colt Dragoon was available in .44-inch caliber, which made it a particularly potent weapon with good stopping power. The six-shot cylinder gave it remarkable flexibility for the time, and it acquitted itself well in use against Indians and Mexicans alike. Its introduction was also well timed for use in the 1849 Gold Rush, when the demand for weapons of self-defense rose alarmingly.

Nobody was going to jump your claim staring down the barrel of a .44 Dragoon. However, the gun did have its drawbacks. Weighing in at a considerable four pounds, two ounces, it was the second-largest Colt revolver ever made. (The Colt Walker was 6 ounces heavier). This weight meant that the gun was supplied with a pommel holster rather than a belt type. Later models also had a shoulder stock, enabling them to be fired like carbines. Many examples were factory-engraved with Texas Ranger and Indian fight scenes, in honor of the gun's pedigree. Despite later advances in pistols, the Dragoon was carried for many years on the frontier. Over 20,000 examples were made.

The Dalton Gang

Opposite page: After the failure of the Coffeyville bank raids, the corpses of Bob and Grat Dalton are held up for the photographer.

Below: Bob Dalton and his sweetheart, Eugenia Moore.

" *The Daltons died without taking their boots off.*"
– Sign placed next to the Daltons' graves

Lewis and Adeline Dalton had a large family of fifteen children; ten boys and five girls. Most of the Dalton offspring were born in Cass County, Michigan, where Lewis owned a saloon, but the family later settled on a farm outside of Coffeyville, Kansas. With no hint of what was to come, the Daltons' eldest son, Frank, became a Deputy U.S. Marshal, working for Judge Isaac Parker in Oklahoma's dangerous Indian Territory. His younger brothers revered him and the whole family were devastated when he was cruelly murdered by outlaw Will Towerly. Already wounded by the horse thief Dave Smith, Frank begged Towerly not to shoot him, saying that he was already dying, but it was no use. He was buried in Coffeyville Cemetery.

Frank's younger brothers, Emmett, Gratton, and Bob followed him into the service, but were soon disillusioned. Emmett described the work that was expected of them: "Grafting – as we of today know the term – was a mild, soothing description of what occurred." There was also some disagreement over unpaid expenses, and the brothers quit. They subsequently became involved in a little cattle rustling and became outlaws, working on the wrong side of the law. This is a pattern that Western gunmen often followed, starting on one side of the law and ending on the other. Having once been identified as wrong-doers, the penalties for law-breaking were so draconian that petty criminals were almost obliged to continue in a life of crime. This is what happened to the Daltons. Bob and the other brothers formed an eight-man gang, recruiting five other criminals to join them: Bill Power, Dick Broadwell, George Newcomb, Charley Pierce, and Charlie Bryant. The gang then began a brief but flamboyant career of train robberies and holdups, ultimately planning to break all records by pulling off a double bank heist in their hometown of Coffeyville. It was Bob Dalton's ambition to "beat anything Jesse James ever did – rob two banks at once, in broad daylight." Targeting their home town was their first mistake.

Above: The Condon Bank at Coffeyville, photographed at the time of the raid.

They rode into town, armed with pearl-handled Colt .45s, disguised as a U.S. Marshal and his posse. Despite wearing false beards, the three Dalton brothers were almost instantly recognized by a passerby, who alerted the marshal and townsfolk. They had planned to rob the First National Bank first, and then go on to the C.M. Condon & Company Bank. Their first raid went off successfully, but as they left the Condon Bank they were met by a hail of bullets from a group of armed citizens led by Marshal Charles T. Connelly. A massive gun battle ensued in which Connelly and three townspeople were killed. After Connelly's demise, liveryman John J. Kloehr took over the attack, and four members of the Dalton gang fell, shot in what is now known as Death Alley. The four gang members killed were Bob and

Grat Dalton, Bill Powers, and Dick Broadwell. Emmett Dalton was very seriously injured, collecting twenty-three gunshot wounds, but – miraculously – he survived.

The bodies of the dead gang members were treated with scant regard, photographed like trophies, and publicly displayed. For years, the two dead Dalton brothers lay in a grave unmarked except for a rusty piece of iron pipe, to which the gang had tethered their horses. Some years later, Emmett erected a headstone for them. He had been sentenced to life imprisonment after the disastrous Coffeyville raids, but was released after serving fourteen years in the Kansas State Penitentiary in Lansing. Emmett went on to lead a blameless life. He moved to California and became a real estate agent, author, and movie actor. In 1909, he was

Above: Bill Powers, Bob and Grat Dalton, and Dick Broadwell lie dead and handcuffed outside Coffeyville Jail on October 5, 1892.

Above: Emmett Dalton survived his incarceration, and appeared in a Hollywood movie about the Dalton brothers.

employed as a consultant on a film about the Dalton gang's last stand, and wrote several books condemning criminality. In 1918, he played himself in the film version of his book *Beyond the Law*. In 1931, Emmett published *When the Daltons Rode*, which was later made into a movie about the gang's brief career. He died six years later in 1937.

The Dodge City Peace Commission

The Dodge City War must be one of the most famous bloodless conflicts in history, and a consequently a strange interlude in the history of Western gunfighters. From its beginnings, Dodge City, Kansas, was known as The Wickedest City in America, and was a hub of gambling, carousing, the whiskey trade, and prostitution. *The Hays Sentinel* said that the town was "full of prostitutes, and every house is a brothel." The so-called Dodge City Gang ran the town on the simple principle that any activity that made money was a good thing. The local merchants and saloonkeepers ran the town for the pleasure of thousands of cowboys that drifted through, and took as much money from them as they could. *The Yates Center News* described the town as "a den of thieves and cutthroats, the whole town in league to rob the unwary stranger." Local saloon keeper James H. Kelley – mayor of Dodge City from 1877 until 1881 – was the leader of the gang, and the Masterson brothers, Charlie Bassett, and Wyatt Earp were his most prominent associates. But in 1881, Mayor B. Webster was elected on a reform ticket to clean up the town. Many townsfolk were sick of the constant brawling, gun fighting, and vice that afflicted Dodge City, and were looking for a more peaceful way of life. Ironically, although Webster had opened a dry goods store in the town in 1872, by the time he was elected mayor he also owned two saloons. His cleanup campaign was really a way of cornering the town's lucrative rackets for himself and his friends. He soon started to substitute prominent Gang members with his own people, replacing city marshal Jim Masterson with one of his bartenders, Fred Singer. Webster then went on to post a series of moral ordinances throughout the town reading, "All thieves, thugs, confidence men, and persons without visible means of support will take notice that the ordinance enacted for their special benefit will be rigorously enforced on and after tomorrow." In reality, Webster used the fines he collected to fund his appointed lawmen and retain his grip on Dodge. He levied fines of $5 to $100 on prostitutes, brothel keepers, vagrants, or those involved in "any unlawful calling whatever," so this was a lucrative source of income.

Luke Short arrived in the town in 1882. Bat Masterson described his five-foot six-inch frame as a "small package, but one of great dynamic force." Short was a well-known gambler, dandy, and man killer, celebrated as the "Undertaker's Friend." He had shot Charlie Storms dead inside the notorious Oriental Saloon in Tombstone. He was also a close friend of Wyatt Earp and Bat Masterson. Short

Above: Timberline, a noted Dodge city prostitute, still displays some of the good looks she had before debauchery, drink, and disease ruined her and many other "soiled doves."

Left: Dodge City advises would-be troublemakers to refrain from carrying firearms in the city limits. Prickly Ash Bitters was a popular alcoholic drink brewed from this aromatic and bitter shrub. It was a favorite "gunfight lubricant."

subsequently bought a half share in Dodge's Long Branch Saloon, but Mayor Webster longed to get this loose cannon out of town and drive him out of business. As far as Webster was concerned, Short was a dangerous business rival with undesirable friends and acquaintances. Supposedly as part of Webster's "cleanup" of the town, Sheriff Louis C. Hartman arrested three "singers" at the Long Branch. Furious, Short tried to spring the women from jail, but ended up in a shootout with Hartman. A few days later, Short was captured by Marshal Jack Bridges, charged with assault, fined $2,000, and deported from the town as an undesirable. He caught a train east to Kansas City, from where he wired his friends to come to his aid. Bat Masterson suggested that Short should go to Topeka to discuss his predicament with Governor George Washington Glick. Glick was an anti-prohibitionist, and was immediately sympathetic to Short's tale of "political differences and business rivalry." When Glick summoned the county clerk of Ford County, W.F. Petillon, to give evidence, he confirmed Short's version of events. On May 15, the *Kansas City Evening Star* published a list of the men who were assembling to facilitate Short's return to Dodge City "and protect him from molestation". They included Wyatt Earp, Doc Holliday, Shotgun Collins, Rowdy Joe Lowe, Bat Masterson, and Charlie Bassett. Dodge's thoroughly intimidated Sheriff Hinkle started to meet all incoming trains from Kansas City with a posse in tow.

Wyatt Earp arrived in Dodge City on May 31, 1883, accompanied by Dan Tipton, Johnny Green, Texas Jack Vermillion, and Johnny Millsap. Bat Masterson's friend and part-time lawman "Prairie Dog" Dave Morrow met the group from the train. Earp persuaded Morrow to swear him and his companions in as deputies so that they could legally wear their guns in town. Morrow obliged. Several more "Peace Commissioners" subsequently arrived to

Above: Luke Short was the proprietor of the famous Elephant Saloon in Fort Worth, Texas, which became the haunt of the most accomplished Western cardsharps.

support their friends, including Charlie Bassett, Frank McLain, and Shotgun Collins. Terrified, Sheriff Hinkle wired Governor Glick, asking him to send militiamen to keep the peace. Glick declined, and Webster now knew that he was in a hopeless position. He summoned Wyatt Earp, who was well known for his reasonableness and even temper, to cut a deal and prevent an all-out gun war in the town. Short reappeared in Dodge on June 4, conspicuously armed with at least three guns, one on each hip and a shotgun in his hand. By now, around fifty men were gathered in the Long Branch Saloon ready to support Luke Short's right to return to Dodge City.

By the time Governor Glick's Adjutant General, Thomas Moonlight, arrived in the town a couple of days later, he thought that the trouble had been greatly exaggerated. By this time, the two sides had reached an amicable accommodation. Gambling and prostitution would continue, but the worst elements would be weeded out. Luke Short would be able to return to his business undisturbed. Bat Masterson arrived in town on June 9, and agreed with Moonlight's assessment of the situation. "If at any time they did 'don the war paint,' it was completely washed off before I reached here."

The bloodless Dodge City War was over without a shot having been fired. Moonlight established "Glick's Guards," a group of men selected from both town factions to keep the future peace in Dodge. But the most lasting souvenir of the occasion was the famous photograph of Short and seven of his most notorious friends, taken by C.S. Fly in June 1883. This gang of eight gunfighters, gamblers, lawmen, and saloon keepers became known as the "Dodge City Peace Commission." Sitting in the front of the picture are Charlie Bassett, Wyatt Earp, Frank McLain, and Neal Brown. Standing at the back are W.H. Harris, Luke Short,

Bat Masterson, and W.F. Petillon. After the picture was taken, the "Commission" dispersed around the country, never to be seen together again.

Unabashed by having been the cause of so much trouble, Luke Short sold his share of the Long Branch saloon in November that year, and moved on to Fort Worth, Texas, where he bought another saloon. Short threatened to sue Dodge City for having forced him to leave the town in 1883, and was awarded an out-of-court settlement by the town. He put the money to good use, became a successful and wealthy professional gambler, and moved into Fort Worth's high society. But he never lost his impetuous streak, and killed the well-known gunfighter Jim Courtright in a February 1887 shootout. But it was illness, not violence, that was to bring about Short's demise just six years later. In 1893, he died of "dropsy" at the Gueda Springs mineral spa, at the ripe old age of thirty-nine. Not even his body was returned to Dodge City, and his wife buried him at Fort Worth.

The Doolin-Dalton Gang

Below: The Rose of Cimarron. A well-known prostitute, she was associated with the Doolin-Dalton Gang.

In 1893, Bill Doolin was to form what was to become one of the most violent and disreputable gangs of the Old West. Of all the bands of robbers and shootists that roamed the West, the Doolin-Dalton gang (also known as the Wild Bunch, the Oklahombres, and the Oklahoma Long Riders after their long duster coats), was to meet the most comprehensively violent end. Between 1892 and 1904, all eleven gang members died from gun wounds administered by lawmen or their agents.

William M. "Bill" Doolin was born in Johnson County, Arkansas in 1858. He was the son of a farmer, but rode west in 1881, working odd jobs until he arrived in Oklahoma Territory. He ended up working as a ranch hand at the H-X ranch on the Cimarron River. Doolin became a skilled cow poke and was equally handy with his six-shooter. It was here that Bill hitched up with the Dalton brothers (who had also worked at the H-X). The men formed an alliance that was to evolve into the Wild Bunch. Doolin had his first serious brush with the law in 1891, while he was working at the Bar X Ranch. He and several other cowhands rode into Coffeyville, Kansas, to celebrate Independence Day with a glass of beer. Unfortunately, as Kansas was a dry state, the local law soon became involved in the party. A shootout broke out when the lawmen tried to confiscate the liquor, and two fell wounded. It was the fulcrum of Doolin's life. Implicated in the shootings, he was a wanted man who lived outside the law for the rest of his life.

Two months after this affray, Bill was already riding with the Dalton brothers, participating with them in numerous train robberies in Indian and Oklahoma Territories, including those at Leliaetta, Red Rock, and Adair. Doolin did not flinch at any kind of violence, and shot a doctor dead during one of these raids. Fortunately for him, Bill did not accompany the Daltons on their ill-fated Coffeyville banks raids of October 5, 1892. Many reasons have been proposed for his omission from the gang that day: Bob Dalton was jealous of his popularity, or thought he was too wild, or Doolin's horse went lame. Whatever the true reason for his absence, the Dalton gang was decimated by the Coffeyville debacle. Bob and Grat Dalton, Bill Powers, and Dick Broadwell were all shot to death, and Emmett Dalton was seriously wounded and captured. Despite this, the remnant of the gang, including Bill Doolin, Bill Dalton, George Newcomb, and Charlie Pierce, immediately continued their campaign of robbery and violence, with a train robbery at Caney, Kansas, just a week later.

The gang immediately started to recruit new members to replace the dead and injured, trawling the area for suitable men. Doolin enlisted Dan Clifton, George Waightman, Roy Daugherty, Alf Sohn, Ol' Yantis, Tulsa Jack Blake, and Bob Grounds to form one of the most prolific bands of outlaws in the West. For three years the gang terrorized the area, robbing from banks, trains, and stagecoaches. On November 1, 1892, the gang raided the Ford County Bank at Spearville, Kansas. This resulted in the first death of the re-formed gang. Ol' Yantis was cornered at his sister's farm in Oklahoma Territory and gunned down by a posse of lawmen. On June 11 the following year, the seeds of Doolin's own destruction were sown when the gang held up the California-New Mexico express just west of Cimarron, Kansas. The raid was successful, netting around $1,000 in silver, but Doolin was shot in the right foot. The wound was to cause him trouble for the rest of his life, and ultimately impeded his final escape.

Above: Bill Doolin, one of the West's most notorious bad men.

But for the moment, the gang became more and more daring, and Doolin got married on March 14, 1893. His bride was Edith Ellsworth of Ingalls, Oklahoma Territory, a preacher's daughter. Whether Edith knew of Bill's colorful career is unknown, but she was to stick with him for the rest of his life, keeping their relationship secret. Bill's romance led him to spend a considerable time in Ingalls, and the gang became popular in the town, using George Ransom's saloon as their headquarters. Gang member George Newcomb also found love in the town with Rose Dunn. Rose was to go down in western legend as the Rose of Cimarron. But the gang's domestic comfort was disturbed on September 1, 1893, when they were cornered in the town by a posse of thirteen men. These enforcers included five U.S. marshals, who had entered the town in two wagons. The marshals were led by Deputy Marshal John Hixon. A fierce gun battle that was to become known as the Battle of Ingalls broke out in which three of the marshals were shot. Deputy Dick

Speed was shot dead instantly, while Deputies Tom Hueston and Lafe Shadley (shot by Bill Dalton) died from their wounds the following day. George Newcomb was also wounded, and pinned down by the firefight. Rose braved the bullets to run Newcomb from the Pierce Hotel, bringing him two ammunition belts and a Winchester rifle. She was also reputed to have fired at the marshals to cover her lover's escape from the town. Several bystanders, including local man Frank Briggs, were also killed, and several more were wounded in the firefight. The marshals called out to Doolin to surrender, but his only reply was to tell them to "go to hell!" A single gang member, Roy Daugherty (also known as Arkansas Tom Jones), was captured and sentenced to fifty years in Guthrie Prison, but the rest of the Wild Bunch escaped unscathed. Dalton and Doolin left town riding a single horse, as Dalton had lost his mount in the battle.

But despite this narrow escape from justice, the gang continued with their thieving. Two more men joined the Wild Bunch in early 1894: William F. Raidler and Little Dick West. On January 3, 1894, the gang began the year with a raid on the post office at Clarkson, Oklahoma Territory. They followed this by robbing the Farmers Citizens Bank at Pawnee and the Santa Fe station at Woodward.

By this time, U.S. Marshal Evett Dumas Nix of Oklahoma Territory was sick and tired of the Wild Bunch's activities and assembled the legendary Three Guardsmen to bring the gang to justice. The famous trio, first brought together in 1889, consisted of Deputy U.S. Marshals Bill Tilghman, Chris Madsen, and Heck Thomas.

Nix's written orders of March 20, 1894 were clear: "I have selected you to do this work, placing explicit confidence in your abilities to cope with those desperados and bring them in – alive if possible, dead if necessary." But even as The Guardsmen started to track the gang down, chasing them across five states, the Wild Bunch continued to cut a swath of mayhem throughout the area. In April, they attempted to rob retired U.S. Deputy Marshal W.H. Carr's store at Sacred Heart, Indian Territory. Carr was shot in the stomach during the raid, but managed to shoot George Newcomb in the shoulder. The gang fled empty-handed. But in May 1894, the gang successfully robbed the bank at Southwest City, Missouri, of $4,000. By this time, Bill Dalton had left the Wild Bunch to start his own gang. He recruited Jim Wallace, Big Asa Knight, Jim Knight, and George Bennett to join him. On May 23, they celebrated with a raid on the First National Bank in Longview, Texas. It was disastrous. On June 8, 1894, the local law successfully trailed the gang to their hideout near Ardmore, Texas. Bill Dalton and two others were shot dead, while the fourth man spent the rest of his life in jail.

The net was also tightening around Bill Doolin and his cohorts. On March 3, 1895, a posse tracked the gang to Rose Dunn's family farm, just outside Ingalls. The Dunn family had never been members of the Wild Bunch, but had harbored them from time to time and fenced stolen goods on their behalf. To encourage their quarry to give themselves up, the deputies threw in a stick of dynamite. The Wild Bunch had an extremely narrow escape, having left the previous day.

Above: An unusual panoramic view of Coffeyville, Kansas. The photograph was taken after the Daltons' infamous bank raids made the town notorious.

On April 3, 1895, the gang pulled off their final raid. It was on the Rock Island train. By an amazing stroke of bad fortune, they were unable to open the train safe, which contained an army payroll of over $50,000. They were reduced to robbing the unfortunate passengers instead. Guardsman Chris Madsen picked up the gang's trail on the following day and found the Wild Bunch camping near Ames, Oklahoma Territory. Tulsa Jack was shot and killed in the ensuing gun fight, but the gang itself was shattered by these events and never reunited.

Under the leadership of Nix, the marshals now resorted to more subtle tactics, posting rewards for the killing or capture of gang members and for information leading to their whereabouts. The strategy worked, and when George Newcomb and Charlie Pierce returned to their refuge at Dunn farm, the Dunn brothers shot and killed both men as they lay asleep in their beds. The fact that George Newcomb was their sister's lover didn't save him. Shattered by this betrayal, Bill Doolin tried to cut a deal with Nix for a light prison sentence for robbery, but Nix refused. Bill was forced to hide out in New Mexico with Little Dick West. But Bill missed Edith and their young son, and returned to Oklahoma to collect his family. The trio then made their way to Kansas. But Marshal Bill Tilghman tracked Edith to their refuge in Eureka Springs, Oklahoma, and after a fist fight in a bathhouse, managed to capture Doolin himself. Taken to Guthrie, Oklahoma, to stand trial, Doolin made good his promise that he

Left: Christopher Madsen was born in Denmark and served in the Danish army before immigrating to the United States. He joined the Fitch Cavalry before becoming a Western lawman.

would never spend time behind bars by organizing a mass break-out for himself and thirty-seven other prisoners on July 5, 1896. He fled to Mexico and hid at writer Eugene Manlove Rhode's ranch. With Doolin out of the way, the surviving gang members scattered far and wide.

Despite Doolin's violent and criminal nature, it was his love for his wife and child that were to be his nemesis. Lonely for their company, he left the relative safety of Mexico to collect Edith from her family's home at Lawson, Oklahoma

Opposite page: Henry Andrew Thomas, known as "Heck." Thomas was one of the famous Three Guardsmen, with Bill Tilghman and Chris Madsen. Together, they helped to establish the rule of law in early Oklahoma.

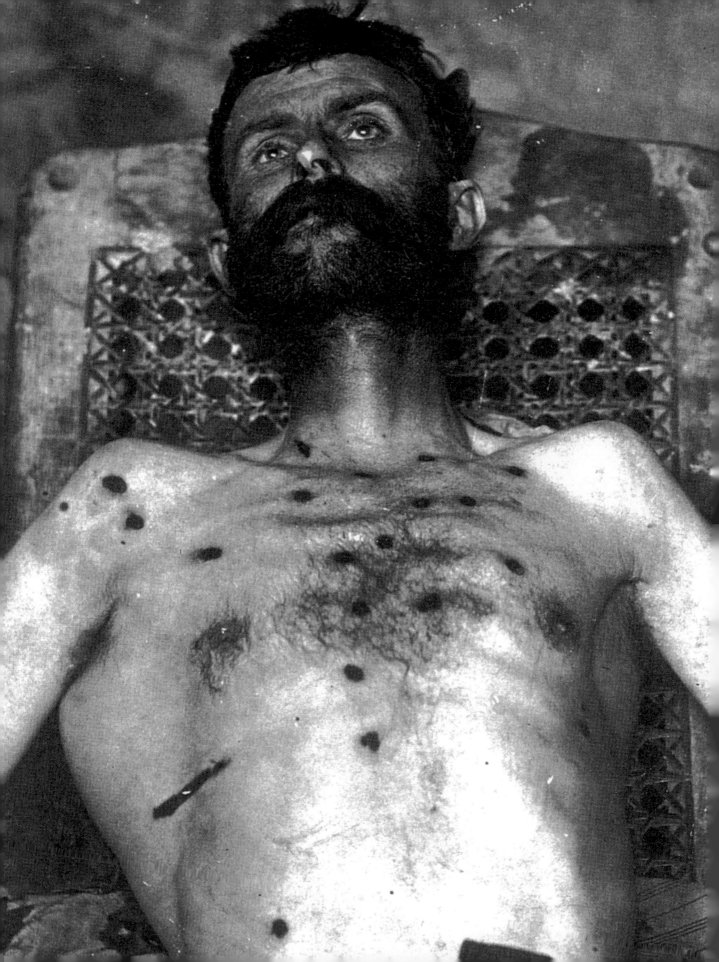

Territory. As he approached the farmhouse on foot, quietly leading his horse, Marshall Heck Thomas and his posse ambushed him. Heck called on Doolin to surrender. Doolin's response was to raise his rifle, and the posse shot it from his hands. Doolin then pulled a six-gun. It was to be his last violent action. Deputies Bill Dunn and Heck Thomas brought him down with a rain of bullets and shotgun fire. It was August 24, 1896. For a man of his chosen profession, Doolin had almost made it to old age.

Even in death, the famous outlaw was allowed no dignity; his corpse was put on show, undressed to the waist to show his fatal injuries. It was really true, the man who had organized a spree of robbery and murder that had terrorized the West had met his own ignominious end.

By the time of Doolin's death, only two other Wild Bunch members were still alive and free: Dynamite Dick Clifton and Little Dick West. Briefly, the pair joined up with the Jennings Gang, but left after a short time with them. Clifton survived until 1897, when he was shot and killed by a posse led by Guardsman Chris Madsen near Checotah, Indian Territory. The following year, Chris Madsen's Marshals also accounted for Little Dick West, in Logan County, Oklahoma Territory, on April 8, 1898. Little Bill Raidler was the final member of the Wild Bunch to meet his maker. Captured by Bill Tilghman, Raidler had been in jail since September 1895. He was paroled for ill health in 1903, but his freedom proved short lived. He died in 1904, from wounds received at the time of his capture.

The ignominious end of the Doolin-Dalton gang was largely the work of U.S. Marshall Nix, who had made their capture and dispersal his top priority. He knew that the West could not accommodate men of this kind and hope to become civilized. As well as his high-profile appointment of the Three Guardsmen, it is estimated that as many as a hundred marshals worked on their capture under Nix's direction. In addition to bringing about the end of a veritable tide of lawless behavior, the destruction of the Wild Bunch sent out a strong message that the age of the criminal gunman's supremacy was drawing to a close in the West.

Opposite page: Bill Doolin lies dead on a mortuary slab, riddled with bullets. He was killed by a posse in Lawson, Oklahoma in 1896.

Colt Buntline Special

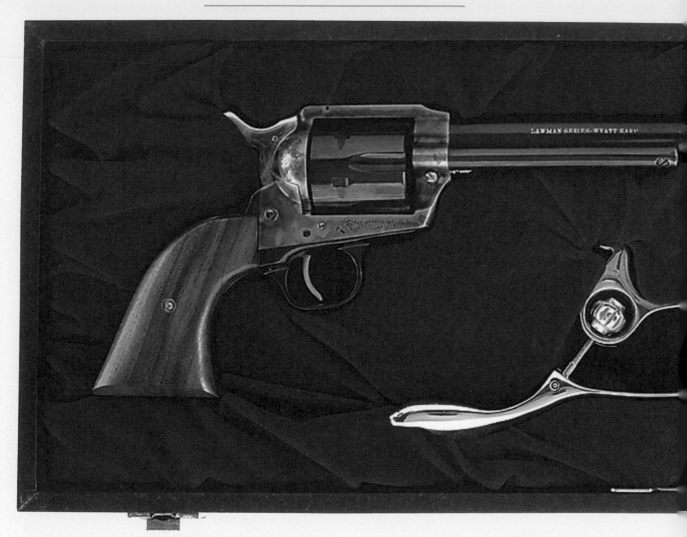

An exciting version of the Colt Single Action appeared at the Philadelphia Centennial Exhibition of 1876, when the weapon was offered with a sixteen-inch barrel and a skeleton shoulder stock. Only thirty examples were originally offered. The gun acquired its legendary association with Wyatt Earp when (it was claimed) dime novelist Ned Buntline (Edward Judson) ordered five Colt Special .45 revolvers to equip the Dodge City Peace Commission, of whom Earp was one. This is how the guns got their name,

the Buntline Specials. It is not known if Earp actually carried his Special, but Buckskin Frank Leslie, a Tombstone gambler and bartender, ordered a ten-inch version in 1881. This was the year of the Earp brothers' famous gunfight at the O.K. Corral.

Clearly these experimental modifications would have turned the Colt Single Action into a very useful weapon. Fired down a sixteen-inch barrel, the .45 cartridges would have been extremely accurate and have had great stopping power at range. The nickel-plated skeleton stock

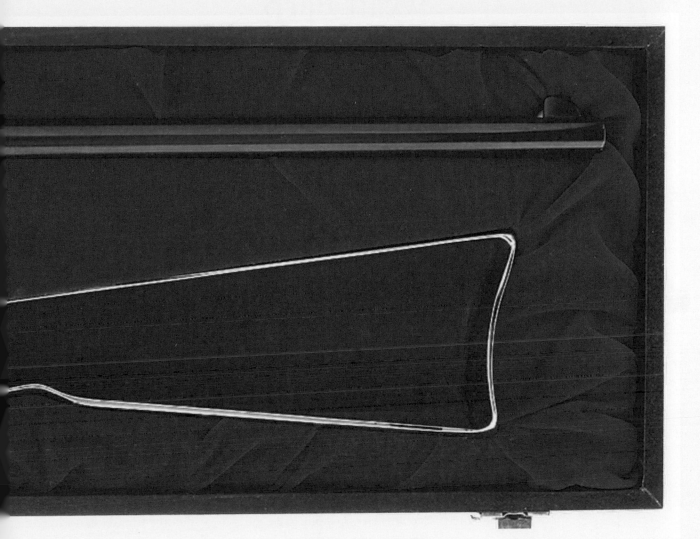

meant that the shootist could hold the gun extremely steady, and take careful aim before squeezing the trigger. The gun could also be fired without the stock, and the extra length and weight of the barrel would have ironed out any tendency to kick. The gun went on to be manufactured for many years after 1876, and is still available in presentation cases like the one shown.

SPECIFICATIONS

Caliber: 0.45

Length of barrel: 16 inches

Barrel shape: Round

Finish: Blue/casehardened

Grips: Walnut

Action: Single Action Revolver

Year of manufacture: 1876

Manufacturer: Colt

Above: A modern reproduction of this legendary arm, complete with skeleton stock and silk lined presentation case. Such weapons are highly prized by collectors.

Wyatt Earp

Below: The Colt Buntline
Special, said to have been
carried by Wyatt Earp.

Wyatt Earp was born in Monmouth, Illinois, and grew up on a farm in Iowa. He became one of the most complex and interesting of the gunfighter frontiersmen of the West. In 1864, Wyatt and his brothers moved to Colton, California, with their parents, which was near San Bernadino. Like many frontier men, Wyatt worked in a succession of "Western" jobs: shotgun messenger for Wells Fargo, railway worker, and buffalo hunter. He also joined several of his contemporaries in law enforcement, including Bat Masterson and Bill Hickok. Wyatt served as a deputy marshal in Wichita, Kansas, and in Dodge City itself. He was reputed to have carried a Colt handgun, either an Army or a Peacemaker. Less reliably, legend has it that he also used a Colt "Buntline Special," with a

detachable stock. This particular weapon may just have been a presentation piece, given to him in the 1920s by an adoring fan. Ned Buntline presented the original Buntlines to various members of the Doge City Peace Commission, but not all of the recipients considered the weapons practical. Personally, Earp was noted as a tough and decisive man, but was also considered by many to be self-contained, a "cold fish." Despite this, he was a lifelong friend of both Bat Masterson and Doc Holliday, who he originally met while working in Kansas. Like many Western gunmen, Wyatt also gained a reputation as a talented professional gambler.

Earp had gone East and married in 1870, but his new wife died suddenly. He remarried and left Dodge City in 1878, setting up home with his brothers and their wives in Tombstone, Arizona. Tombstone was then a boom silver mining town, originally founded in 1877. Known as "the town too tough to die," it seemed an ideal location for the family. In dress and manner, the Earp brothers exemplified the gentlemen gunmen of their era; they were hard as nails but poised and stylish. Wyatt subsequently acquired the gambling concession in the town's Oriental Saloon, and his brother Virgil became Town Marshal. Brother Morgan worked for

Left: Wyatt Earp fought in the most famous shootout of all time, the O.K. Corral.

the local police department. Earp's second marriage failed, and he met his third wife, Josephine Marcus, in Tombstone. But everything in town wasn't rosy. A feud developed between the Earp brothers and Ike Clanton's Gang that culminated on October 26, 1881, with the most famous gunfight of them all, just outside the O.K. Corral, where the Earp brothers "swapped lead" with the Clanton-McLaury Gang. Although three men died at the O.K. Corral, the Earp brothers survived the shootout. But in the following year, Morgan Earp was gunned down by an unknown assassin. Predictably, his death was avenged by the surviving Earp brothers, and Wyatt was obliged to skip town to Colorado to avoid being tried for murder. Despite this, Wyatt remained in law enforcement. In 1893, he became a member of the so-called Dodge City Peace Commission (together with Bat Masterson and Charlie Bassett, among others), which convened to support fellow gunslinger and saloon owner Luke Short. The city fathers of Dodge City wanted

Right: Bader &
Laubner's saloon at
Dodge City in the
1880s, complete with a
polished wood bar and
huge plate glass
mirrors.

to clean up the town and make it more attractive to settlers, so they tried to evict undesirable elements like Short and his ilk. They soon backed down when Luke's friends turned up.

Wyatt and Josie spent the next few years tramping around the booming mining towns of the frontier, gambling and investing in real estate and saloons as they passed through. In 1897 they operated a saloon in Alaska at the peak of the gold rush there, and made a fortune estimated at around $80,000. They then headed for Tonopah, Nevada, cashing in on that town's gold strike.

Earp ultimately took up prospecting himself and staked many claims in the Mojave Desert, including several just outside Death Valley. At one stage, he was reputed to have sold a worked-out silver mine for $30,000. In 1906, Earp struck seams of both gold and copper, and spent the final winters of his life working these veins. In the summers he and Josie lived (in some style) in Los Angeles, mixing with the Hollywood glitterati of the time.

Wyatt died in Los Angeles in 1929, at the ripe old age of eighty. He was one of the very few gunslingers to make it into old age, and was perhaps unique in that he was able to enjoy his own burgeoning reputation. He was an intensely paradoxical man, one who had both upheld and manipulated the law: a speculator and gambler, who was also an able businessman and investor who knew the value of hard work. He was a loyal friend and partner who inspired great devotion from his friends, but was also noted for his cool demeanor and lack of personal warmth.

Like all the old gunslingers, he had his own tricks of the trade. Earp claimed that he only ever loaded five bullets into a six-shooter to "ensure against accidental discharge."

Robert Ford

Rober or "Bob" Ford has the unenviable distinction among Western gunfighters of being defined for posterity by the man he murdered; the far more celebrated Jesse James.

Best known as "the dirty little coward," Robert Newton Ford was born in 1861 in Ray County, Missouri. From childhood, Robert hero-worshiped Jesse James, reading the nickel novels he inspired. Bob finally got to meet James in 1880. He and his older brother Charles began to hang around on the outer circle of the remnant of the James-Younger Gang. By this time, several members had been gunned down and captured, so Jesse was probably glad to have the two Fords. Charles was one of six gang members that perpetrated the James-Younger Gang's final train robbery at Blue Cut, where they took around $3,000 in cash and jewelry from the passengers. Robert did not take part in any specific crimes, but was happy to mind the gang's horses and stand-by to help. At this time, the Fords were living with the James family in St. Joseph, Missouri, passing themselves off as Jesse's cousins. Jesse then invited the Ford brothers to join him in what was to be his final crime. He planned to raid the Platte City Bank, and set himself up as a gentleman farmer.

But things began to take a terrible turn in January 1882 when two wanted James Gang members took refuge in the farmhouse home of the Ford brothers' sister, Martha Bolton. This pair of bandits, Wood Hite and Dick Liddel, fell into a quarrel about Martha's favors and drew their weapons. Robert Ford was friendly with Liddel and promptly shot Hite (a cousin of the James brothers') in the head. Missouri's newly elected Governor, Thomas T. Crittenden, brought Ford in to answer for the murder. Fearful of being hanged, and mindful that the governor

Above: Bob Ford poses with the Colt Peacemaker that he used to gun down Jesse James. He was to meet the same fate on June 8, 1892, at the hands of Edward O'Kelley.

Above: Dick Liddell plotted to kill Jesse James. He is armed with a Whitney Navy pistol.

had offered a huge reward for the capture of Jesse James, Ford told Kansas City police commissioner Henry Craig that he could deliver the outlaw to him, alive or dead. Craig was sick of the James brothers' criminality and was determined to eradicate them. On January 13, 1882, Ford cut a deal with the governor for a pardon for the murder of Wood Hite and the reward of $10,000 to capture or assassinate Jesse James. No doubt he also hoped to make a name for himself as the man who brought Jesse James to justice.

In the 2007 movie *The Assassination of Jesse James by the Coward Robert Ford*, Jesse James is portrayed as being anxious and depressed at this time, aware that his luck is running out fast. He feels completely surrounded by federal agents, Pinkerton men, and the sheriffs and marshals of the West. Bizarrely, he seems to cultivate a friendship with Robert Ford, even though he is fully aware that Ford can't be trusted. By this stage, he may also have a suspicion that Ford had killed his cousin, Wood Hite. As the men discussed the upcoming raid on the Platte City Bank, in the James family home, Jesse uncharacteristically put down his gun belt on a

Below: The South East Plaza, Las Vegas, New Mexico, in 1881. Cattle roamed freely between the saloons and gambling dens.

Colt Peacemaker

Below: The model shown was manufactured in 1896 and has the 4¾-inch barrel option, and its own original buscadero-style holster.

No weapons appraisal of the gunfighters could be considered complete without the Colt Peacemaker, or Single Action Army Revolver as it was more properly called. Along with the Winchester 1873, the Colt Peacemaker became famous as "the gun that won the West." Both models were deliberately marketed to use the same ammunition, namely .44-40. This version was marketed as the Colt Frontier Six Shooter. This meant that it was only necessary to carry one type of shell, a self-contained center-fire cartridge. The two guns presented the all-around flexibility of a repeating rifle for long-range work, with the quick-shot revolver for use at short range. Both had outstanding stopping power, provided by the large caliber ammunition.

But the Colt was tremendously expensive at $17 (around $700 today). Back in 1874, this would have been about a month's wages for the average cowhand. Despite its high price, the gun would have been a good investment for a professional outlaw, gunfighter, or lawman.

Interestingly, the Peacemaker was not Samuel Colt's own design, as he died in 1862. This was well before the advent of the center-fire ammunition that made the 1873 revolver so effective. However, it can certainly be argued that Colt's powerful vision for revolving firearms continued to influence his company for many years after his death. After all, as the popular saying went, "God made man, but Colonel Colt made them equal."

The featured example was the property of the Sheriff of Magdalena, New Mexico. It has its original handmade single-loop buscadero holster, decorated with brass tacks and braided rawhide edging. Many guns of this type have been handed down in families for generations.

SPECIFICATIONS

Caliber: 44-40 and .45 Colt

Length of barrel: 3, 4¾, 5 ½, and 7½ inches

Barrel shape: Round

Finish: Blue or Nickel plate

Grips: Hard Rubber

Action: Single

Year of manufacture: 1873 to the present (with a gap from 1941-55)

Manufacturer: Colt's PT.F.A MFG. CO., Hartford, Connecticut

chair to straighten a crooked picture. Robert Ford took this opportunity to shoot the unarmed outlaw in the back of the head. The brothers then ran into town to telegraph the good news to Governor Crittenden and claim their reward. It was at this point that everything started to go horribly wrong for the brothers. They were immediately arrested, tried, and sentenced for murder for James's death, before Crittenden pardoned them. Shaken, they were grateful to be given just a small portion of the massive reward they had been promised.

The Ford brothers' life became completely nightmarish. Forced to act out their betrayal of James nightly in a touring stage show, Charles Ford fell ill with tuberculosis and became addicted to morphine. Worn down by remorse and self-loathing, he committed suicide on May 4, 1884. Bob Ford was reduced to making a living by posing for photographs as the "man who killed Jesse James" in dime museums. Later in 1884, Ford and Dick Liddel opened a saloon in Las Vegas, New Mexico, but Ford was forced to leave the town as he became the target for every would-be assassin in town. He was obliged to wander around the West, trying to stay alive. He survived another murder attempt in Kansas City and moved on to Walsenberg, Colorado, where he opened another saloon. When prospectors discovered silver in Creede, Colorado, Bob moved his business there. He opened Ford's Exchange on May 29, 1892. Six days later it was burned to the ground (supposedly by the Soapy Smith Gang), so the resilient Ford opened a tent saloon in the town until he could rebuild. But just three days later, on June 8, 1892, Edward O'Kelley strolled into his business with a sawn-off shotgun. "Hello, Bob" he called out to Ford, who turned around to see who it was. Kelley discharged both barrels into Ford, killing him instantly. O'Kelley himself became notorious as the "man who killed the man who killed Jesse James." He was pardoned for Ford's murder, but was to meet a similar fate himself. In January 1904, he was gunned down in a shootout with an officer of the law.

Patrick 'Pat' Garrett

Like Bob Ford, Pat Garrett's historical reputation largely rests on the identity of one of his "kills." In his case, it was the July 14, 1881, shooting of Billy the Kid. But in every other respect – background, intelligence, and caliber – the two men were completely different.

Patrick Floyd Jarvis Garrett was born in Cusseta Chambers County, Alabama, on June 5, 1850. He was one of seven children born to John and Elizabeth Garrett. When he was three years old his father bought a plantation in Louisiana, near

Below: The dapper Pat Garrett was elected sheriff and ordered to hunt down Billy the Kid. He shot the twenty-one-year-old dead in a darkened bedroom on the night of July 14, 1881.

Above: Like many famous Westerners, Pat Garrett worked as a buffalo hunter for a few years.

Haynesville and the Arkansas state line, and Pat and his siblings were brought up there. Garrett grew up to be strikingly tall, with a spare frame and an intelligent face. He was nicknamed "Long John," or "Juan Largo." Pat left home in 1869 to work as a Texas cowpuncher on the LS ranch in Dallas County. Part of his job was to control cattle rustling, and so he soon became adept at handling firearms. But Garrett soon tired of life on the range, and left the LS to join his partner W. Skelton Glenn as a buffalo hunter. Unfortunately, the hot-tempered Garrett fell into a quarrel with a fellow hunter over some hides. The man came at him with a hatchet, and Garrett ended up by shooting him. Legend has it that, as he lay dying, the hunter asked Garrett to forgive him, and brought his killer to tears. Forced to lay low for a while, Pat drifted to New Mexico in 1878 and got work as a cowhand on

Peter Maxwell's ranch. Although the ranch was to play an important part in Garrett's future, he once more tired of the cowboy life and left it to work as a bartender at Beaver Smith's Saloon in Fort Sumner. It was while he was working at the saloon that he met the three people who were to be the greatest influences in his life. In 1879, he met and married a local girl, Juanita Gutierrez, but she sickened and died within a year of their marriage. The following year, 1880, he married Juanita's sister, Apolonaria. This union was far more successful, and the couple went on to have nine children together. The third person Garrett met at the saloon was Billy the Kid. The two men struck up a close saloon friendship, gambling together so often that they became known as "Big Casino" and "Little Casino."

This cozy relationship was to come to a crashing end. In November 1880 Garrett was appointed Sheriff of Lincoln County. The area had only just recovered from the infamous Lincoln County wars, but was still plagued with violent rival gangs. Garrett was charged with bringing law and order to the area, and one of the first tasks he was given was to capture jail escapee Henry McCarty, better known to Garrett as his friend "Little Casino." Governor Lew Wallace saw Billy as a menace to the peace and personally offered a reward of $500 for his capture. The relentless Garrett confronted Billy's gang just a few weeks after his appointment, as they rode into Fort Sumner. He shot and killed gang member Tom O'Folliard, but the rest of the gang escaped, including Billy. Garrett tracked them down again less than a week later at Stinking Springs, New Mexico. A second gang member, Charlie Bowdre, was killed in an exchange of gunfire, and Billy himself was captured. Convicted for his many crimes, Billy was incarcerated in the Lincoln County jail, but in April 1881, he managed to escape by killing two guards, J.W. Bell and Bob Olinger. Three months later, Garrett had tracked him down again, this time to the ranch of his old friend Peter Maxwell.

Garrett's version of the events around Billy's subsequent demise was that the Kid came into the room where he was talking to Maxwell, asking *"Quien es? Quien es?"* Garrett immediately discharged two shots, one of which lodged just above the

Below: Billy the Kid's friend Tom O'Folliard. He was killed in a gunfight with Garrett's posse.

Colt Frontier

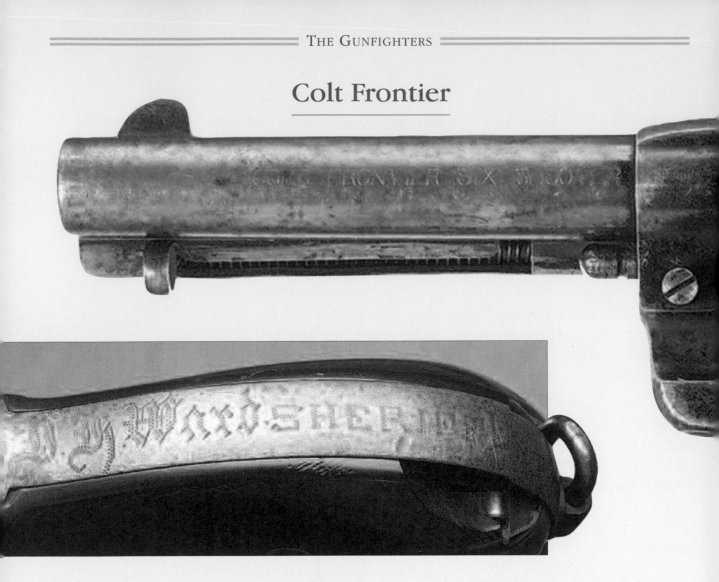

Above: The owner's name, J. H. Ward, is emblazoned on the back strap. Ward was the Sheriff of Vinta, Colorado.

The Colt Frontier was launched in 1878 at the height of the action in the West. Popular calibers were .44–40 and .45-inch, with the barrel available in various lengths. Shorter barrels were more easily concealed and were therefore of interest to plainclothes lawmen and criminals alike. The gun was a double-action revolver allowing for rapid fire. It was an improved version of the Colt Lightning, on which it was based, with a larger frame and sturdier components. The gun is instantly recognizable by the disc on the side of the frame, just behind the cylinder. It was popular with a number of Western

SPECIFICATIONS

Caliber: 0.44-40

Length of barrel: 4¾ inches

Barrel shape: Round

Finish: Blue/gray mixed with surface rust

Grips: Hard Rubber

Action: Double

Year of manufacture: 1878-1905

Manufacturer: Colt

The design of the Frontier really set the pace for Colt revolvers for the next 100 years.

characters, including Pawnee Bill Lilly who taught his wife May to become a crack shot using the gun. Rose Dunn, "The Rose of Cimarron," who was involved with the Doolin Gang, also favored the Frontier. She is cradling the gun lovingly in her most famous portrait.

The featured weapon is a .44–40-inch caliber version of the model and is engraved "J.H. Ward. Sheriff, Vinta CO." on the back strap. Ward was Sheriff of the town from 1886 to 1912, and was responsible for capturing and bringing in Butch Cassidy. Significantly, he was also a party to Cassidy's parole.

Above: Pat Garrett, John W. Poe, and James Brent. They were the sheriffs of Lincoln County between 1877 and 1881.

Kid's heart. Another, much less credible version of the killing, in which Garrett tied up Paulita Maxwell in her bedroom, lured Billy into the room, and killed him with a single blast from his Colt Frontier, was also widely circulated.

Although most people were delighted to see the back of Billy, the manner of his dispatch did not enhance Garrett's reputation. Shooting an unarmed friend, without warning, was not considered true to the code of the Western gunman. Although Sheriff Garrett was the hero of the hour, most people saw his treatment of Billy as cowardly. He lost his re-election campaign for sheriff and never received Governor Wallace's reward.

Disgusted by this lack of gratitude, Pat turned to ranching and collaborated with his friend Ash Upson on a book about Billy entitled *The Authentic Life of Billy the Kid, the Noted Desperado of the Southwest*. As eight other books had already been published on McCarty, Garrett's book sold badly.

Over the next few years, Garrett tried and failed to re-enter law enforcement and public life in several different roles: as Sheriff of Grant County, New Mexico, state senator, and Sheriff of Chaves County. He briefly joined the Texas Rangers, but left the service after only a few weeks.

It was 1896 when Garrett was finally appointed as a sheriff once more, in Dona Ana County. He was confirmed in the position with an election in January the following year. This was largely because the governor felt that his help was required to solve the case of the disappearance and probable murder of Colonel Fountain and his eight-year-old son, Henry. The main suspects were local lawmen William McNew, James Gililland, and Oliver M. Lee. Although Garrett's posse finally caught up with Lee and Gilliland in July 1898, he was unable to capture them and one of his deputies was killed in a shootout with the accused men. Later, Lee and Gilliland surrendered and were tried for the murder of the two Fountains. But in the absence of the bodies, they were acquitted.

In 1901, Garrett's luck turned again. President Theodore Roosevelt was fascinated by stories of the gunfighters of the Old West, and became friendly with several famous Westerners, including Pat Garrett. In December that year, he appointed Garrett as his customs collector in El Paso, Texas. Garrett retained the post until 1905, but at that point, Roosevelt refused to reappoint him to the job. Garrett's close friendship with a man called Tom Powers, who was reputed to have beaten his own father into a coma, had damaged his reputation. Despite a face-to-face meeting with the President, Garrett failed to change Roosevelt's mind.

Bitterly, he returned to his ranch in the San Andres Mountains of New Mexico, but new problems started to pile in on him. He owed substantial taxes and was being held responsible for a defaulted loan that he had co-signed for his friend. Debts began to pile up and he owed money to many people in the local area.

Realizing that he needed to do something drastic, Garrett decided to sell his ranch. After some difficult negotiations with local rancher Carl Adamson, the pair cut a deal for Garrett's property. Unfortunately, Garrett's misfortunes didn't end there. He had leased part of his land to goat farmer Jesse Wayne Brazel, who now

Right: Pat's son, Jarvis Garrett, marked the location of his father's shooting death.

held him to ransom for his cooperation in allowing the deal with Adamson to go through. After a heated discussion between the three men in Las Cruces, Garrett and Adamson were riding back along the San Augustin Pass when the irate Brazel caught up with them on horseback. In court Brazel maintained that, in the ensuing argument, Garrett leaned forward to pick up his double-barreled shotgun, so he shot him first in "self-defense," fatally wounding the lawman in the head and stomach. Adamson verified his story and Brazel was acquitted. This was a typical end for a man with a gunslinging reputation; they inspired so much fear that their adversaries were minded to shoot first, rather than take their chances in a fair fight.

Garrett's remains were laid out in the undertaker's parlor, and dozens came to see the mortal remains of the man who had gunned down Billy the Kid. His body was too tall for any pre-made coffin, so an especially long one had to be shipped in from El Paso.

Garrett's funeral service was held on March 5, 1908, and he was buried next to his daughter Ida (who had died eight years earlier) in the Masonic Cemetery in Las Cruces. His son, Jarvis Garrett, marked the location of his father's shooting in the 1930s, and the site is now protected by an organization known as the Friends of Pat Garrett.

John Wesley Hardin

*" The man who does not exercise the first law of nature –
that of self preservation – is not worthy of living and
breathing the breath of life."*

*"I had no mercy on men whom I knew only wanted to
get my body to torture and kill."* – John Wesley Hardin

*Oh I'm a good ol' rebel, now that's just what I am
For this fair land of Freedom, I do not give a damn,
I'm glad I fit against it, I only wish we'd won,
And I don't want no pardon for anything I've done.*
– Confederate Civil War song

Above: John Wesley Hardin became the most feared gunfighter in Texas. He claimed to have gunned down forty-four men, but his tally was more likely to have been twenty.

Unlike almost all Western gunmen, John Wesley ("Wes") Hardin was largely a professional manslayer. His nicknames and epithets are proof enough of the fear that he inspired. He was known as "the meanest man in Texas," "the dark angel of Texas," and "a homicidal desperado."

In common with several other Western bad men, John's father, James G. Hardin, was a preacher who named his son after the founder of the Methodist faith. Hardin was born on May 26, 1853, in Bonham, Texas. His mother was Mary Elizabeth Dixon Hardin. In his autobiography, her son described her as being "blond, highly cultured… charity predominated in her disposition." The family did not have a settled home; they were Texas wayfarers who drifted from the home of one relative to another. Despite this, the Hardin parents were highly respected in the various communities in which they lived. But from a very early age it was obvious that John had an extremely violent temper and vengeful nature. He was almost expelled from his father's own school for attacking another boy, John Sloter, with a knife when he was fourteen. By the age of just fifteen he had made his first kill. His victim was a black ex-slave known as Mage. In later life, Hardin justified his flight from justice by saying that "To be tried at that time for the killing of a Negro meant certain death at the hands of a court backed by Northern bayonets." It is alleged that he killed three Texas Rangers as they tried to bring him in. This was to

Above: Abilene in 1879. The town was a mixture of brick-built and false-fronted wooden buildings.

Opposite page: A tintype
of John Wesley Hardin,
made at Abilene in 1871.

set up a pattern, and Wes Hardin was to kill several more black men over his "career." It is very likely that he saw freed slaves as the embodiment of the ignominious defeat of the South. By the age of seventeen Hardin had become a professional gambler, duelist, sometime follower of the Klu Klux Klan, and all round bad man. Gambling was to influence the balance of his life, and he reveled in his sobriquet "Young Seven-up," that referred to one of his favorite card games. Wes had also evolved an unusual way of carrying his pistols which he believed gave his draw the edge of speed. His holsters were sewn into his vest, with the butts pointed inwards, across his chest. This meant that he crossed his arms to draw, and he practiced this maneuver every day. The tide of killings in which he was involved continued. Among others, he shot gambler Jim Bradley to death in 1869; a man who tried to rob him in Kosse, Texas; Waco City Marshal L.J. Hoffman; and Jim Smally of the Texas police.

During this time, when he was constantly on the run for some murder or other, Wes worked as a cowboy on the cattle drives, including the Chisholm Trail. In 1871, he met Wild Bill Hickok in Abilene, Texas, where Hickok was Town Marshal. In his autobiography, Hardin wrote "I have seen many fast towns but I think Abilene beat them all." The two gunmen became friends of a sort; Hardin was delighted to be seen in the company of the celebrated gunfighter and Hickok treated the younger man as a protégé. But after Hardin shot and killed a stranger in the adjacent hotel room for snoring, Hickok realized that his friend was deranged, and vowed to punish him. Hardin knew that Hickok would show him no quarter and fled the town. "If Wild Bill found me in a defenseless condition, he would… kill me to add to his reputation."

Soon after this ignominious departure, Hardin was reunited with the Clements branch of his family. But trouble seemed to follow him around. In 1872, he was shot by Phil Sublett during a poker game and seriously injured. He temporarily surrendered himself to Sheriff Dick Reagan, but thought better of it and escaped from Gonzales jail. This short brush with the justice system did not subdue Hardin's violent temper. In 1873 he shot Dewitt County Sheriff Jack Helm, and on May 26, 1874, he celebrated his twenty-first birthday by shooting Texas Deputy Sheriff Charles Webb of Brown County. It was for this crime that Hardin was finally brought to justice, and his killing of Webb also had a devastating effect on his family. The outraged citizens of Brown County formed a lynch mob to take their revenge on anyone associated with Webb's killer. Hardin's parents, wife, brother Joseph, and two male cousins, Tom and Bud Dixon, were taken into protective

custody in the local jail. But this did not save them. The mob broke in and hung Joseph Hardin and the two Dixon brothers. It was said that the posse cut the hanging ropes deliberately long so that the men died a slow and agonizing death of strangulation.

A price of $4,000 was put on Hardin's head for the murder of Webb. Undercover Texas Ranger Jack Duncan finally caught up with Hardin, who was living under an assumed name of James W. Swain, on a train in Pensacola, Florida. For once in his life, Hardin's draw failed, as his pistols got caught in his suspenders. He was finally arrested in 1877. Convicted of Webb's murder, Wes was sentenced to twenty-five years in Huntsville prison in Texas. He served nearly seventeen years in jail, during which time he battled with ill health and was bed-ridden for two years. But he also took his enforced seclusion as an opportunity to study theology and law.

Hardin's wife, Jane Bowen Hardin, had died during his time in prison, on November 6, 1892. So when he received an early pardon from Governor Hogg in 1894, he was released as a forty-one-year-old widower with three grown-up children. Pardoned in 1895, Hardin passed his law exams and obtained a license to practice. The following year he married the fifteen-year-old "Callie" Lewis, but the marriage was soon over.

In 1895, Hardin moved to El Paso, and worked as a lawyer while writing his autobiography, *The Life of John Wesley Hardin as Written by Himself.* On March 30 of that year, the *El Paso Herald* announced that "John Wesley Hardin, at one time one of the most noted characters in Texas, is in the town."

But Hardin's personality had not improved during his time in jail. He committed his final murder, of an innocent Mexican man in El Paso, for a $5 bet. He was also gambling again. In May 1985, he took back $95 he had lost in a dice game at gunpoint, and was subsequently fined $25 for "unlawfully carrying a pistol."

Hardin's return to his old ways of squabbling and disputatious behavior was to be his undoing. Hardin started an affair with one of his married women clients and unwisely boasted that he had hired two local lawmen, Jeff Milton and George Scarborough, to kill her husband, Martin McRose. Mrs. McRose herself was then arrested by El Paso lawman John Selman Jr. for "brandishing a gun in public." Hardin became involved in a verbal brawl with Selman and his father John Selman Sr. on the afternoon of August 19, 1895. Later that day, Hardin visited the town's Acme Saloon Bar and began shooting dice with local furniture dealer Henry Brown. Selman Sr. came in, saw Hardin, and shot him in the head. Although this bullet killed Hardin instantly, Selman pumped a further three shots into his lifeless body, as though he could hardly believe that the notorious man killer lay dead on the floor. Legend has it that Hardin's last words were, "Four sixes to beat, Henry."

The most deadly gunfighter in American history was shot down like a dog at the age of forty-two. Selman was acquitted of the crime. When he died, Hardin was carrying a .38 caliber, two-and-a-half inch barrel Colt Model 1877 Lightning revolver with mother-of-pearl grips (serial number 84304). The gun had been presented to him by a grateful client and was shipped from the Colt factory in 1891. Unfortunately for him, Wes Hardin never got a chance to draw it from its tooled leather holster, bought in El Paso. His previous gun had also been a Colt revolver; an 1877 .41 caliber Thunderer. He had used this gun to hold up and rob the Gem Saloon.

Over his short and violent career, Hardin claimed to have killed at least forty men, although he always maintained that he didn't kill anyone who didn't need killing. This certainly wasn't the case. Even by the standards of his type, Hardin was a violent and capricious murderer who killed men for little or nothing; maybe just because he had made a bet to do so, or because he hated the color of their skin. In the end, his death can only be viewed as poetic justice.

Hardin's unfinished autobiography was published in 1896, the year after his death.

Winchester Model 1887 Lever Action Shotgun

The 1887 Shotgun was hardly the most elegant of the company's weapons.

In the final years of the Frontier, many weapons evolved into more deadly versions of earlier arms. Gone was the primitive percussion system, which took time to load, and muzzle-loaders that suffered from variable powder charges and poor gas sealing. Center-fire brass cartridges and double action had made the revolver a much more serious weapon. Outlaws like Billy the Kid quickly caught on to the latest models, such as the Colt Lightning and Frontier-type revolvers. Rifles with reliable repeating mechanisms were also available. Similarly, shotgun design had to move with the times.

In gunfights, a shotgun was often needed to pin down opposing forces of overwhelming strength. Shotguns also appeared in the role of protecting jails or bullion shipments, where their close-range devastation would deter potential hold-ups. But they suffered from the serious drawback of having only a two-shot capacity in double-barrel form. Colt had developed an early version of a revolving shotgun, but this never really took off. It was left to Winchester to develop a lever-action shotgun to reflect their successful rifles. Designed by John Browning, the 1887 shotgun was chunky and aggressive-looking, just right for a weapon designed to intimidate. It had a five-shot magazine in a tube positioned under the barrel, and was available in 10 and 12-gauge. The barrel lengths of the gun ranged from thirty-two inches to a "sawn-off" twenty inches for crowd control (or criminal) purposes.

The gun was a favorite weapon with the Texas Rangers, and it continued in production until 1920. A weapon of this kind was used by Texan lawman George W. Scarborough, who killed the assassin of John Wesley Hardin, John Selman, in an alley. Scarborough died following a shootout in Deming, New Mexico, in 1900. These were violent times indeed.

Above: Close-up of the familiar Winchester underlever action and 5-shot magazine tube slung under the barrel.

SPECIFICATIONS

Caliber: 12-Gauge

Length of barrel: 28 inches

Barrel shape: Round

Finish: blue/casehardened

Grips: Walnut

Action: 5 shot lever action

Year of manufacture: 1887

Manufacturer: Winchester
   Repeating Arms Co.,
   New Haven, Connecticut

Wild Bill Hickok

Above: Wild Bill Hickok was a lifelong dandy. Here, he wears his trademark black frock coat and silk neckerchief. On the opposite page, he is dressed for his appearance with Buffalo Bill Cody's theatrical troupe in 1873.

To this day, the reputation of Wild Bill Hickok epitomizes that of the gun-fighting lawman; he was a "genuine lover of law and order," as well as a great showman and latter day duellist.

Hickok was born in Troy Grove, Illinois in 1837. In 1855 Bill joined General Jim Lane's "Free State Army," where he first met the young William Cody. His prominent nose and upper lip earned him the nickname "Duck Bill," but he referred to himself as "Wild Bill" and it stuck. In 1858 Bill became one of the first four constables of Monticello Township, Kansas. Having been seriously injured by a bear, Bill was sent to Rock Creek Station, Nebraska to recuperate. It was here in 1861 that the twenty-four-year-old Bill shot and killed David McCanles in a shootout. He was tried for murder, but was judged to have acted in self defense.

When the Civil War broke out, Hickok joined the Union army as a teamster and had risen to being a wagon master by the time he was discharged in 1862. Reputedly, he went on to spy and scout for the army. After the war he returned to the law. But on July 21, 1865 all that nearly came to an end when he shot and killed Davis Tutt Jr. in a "quick draw" shootout in Springfield, Missouri. The pair had quarrelled over a gold watch. This famous gunfight was the first recorded prototype of what was to become the classic gunfight of western legend. Again, Hickok was brought to justice, but acquitted on the basis that he had shot Tutt in self defense in a "fair fight." Many disagreed.

In 1866 he became Marshal of Fort Riley, Kansas. This was the time of the Indian Wars, and in 1867 Bill was attacked by a large group of Indians while scouting on the Great Plains. He killed two of the braves, and the others retreated and let him pass. In the following year, Bill took off to Niagara Falls to try his hand at acting in the revue *The Daring Buffalo Chases of the Plains.* Unfortunately, Bill proved to be a terrible actor, and in 1868, he returned to the law as Marshal of Hays, Kansas, sometimes working alongside Bill Cody as a scout. After an eventful time in Hays,

Above: Two dead cavalrymen, gunned down by Bill Hickok at Hays City in 1870.

Hickok was invited to become Town Marshal of Abilene, Texas, in 1871. Most of his predecessors in the job now lay in Boot Hill cemetery. They included the previous incumbent, pacifist Marshal Tom "Bear River" Smith, who had been murdered by an axe-wielding homesteader in November 1870. Not unreasonably, the weary citizens felt that a "noted" and feared individual like Hickok would stand a better chance of keeping the peace, particularly during the annual spring cattle drives. These generally resulted in the town being completely torn up by lawless cowboys. In fact, Hickok's reputation wasn't entirely deserved. He was a tremendous self-publicist who actively propagated the fiction that he had killed over a hundred white men. His real lifetime tally was actually closer to forty. Once installed as town marshal, he proceeded to clean up the town, running Abilene from a card table in the Long Branch Saloon, and earning a massive $150 a month for his services. One cowboy described him as looking like a "mad old bull," and he made every attempt to look as intimidating as possible. His habitual costume consisted of a black frock coat, a low-brimmed black hat, and two ivory-butted and silver-mounted pistols thrust behind a red silk sash. He wore the pistol handles reversed, "cavalry-style," to speed his draw. His favourite weapons were two silver-plated Colt 1851 .36 Navy pistols, engraved "J.B. Hickok-1869," and he carried these weapons until his death.

Hickok's larger-than-life presence in Abilene succeeded in keeping a lid on much of the town violence. He was also surprisingly successful in bringing gun control to the town, disarming even reluctant Texans. He posted a notice that disarmament would be vigorously enforced, and the *Abilene Chronicle* reported this. Their editorial comment ran: "There's no bravery in carrying revolvers in a civilized community. Such a practice is well enough and perhaps necessary when among Indians or other barbarians, but among white people it ought to be discountenanced."

Above: Wild Bill Hickok, photographed at Rolla, Missouri, in 1864 or 1865. At the time, he was a contract scout for the Union.

As marshal, Hickok was also responsible for street cleaning, and kept the town roads clear of dead dogs and horses. He was paid a bonus of fifty cents for every stray dog he shot. On one occasion, he was called upon to dispatch a mad Texas longhorn that was rampaging through the town. Hickok greatly enjoyed his time in Abilene, rooming with a succession of prostitutes, gambling, and drinking heavily. The famous painter N.C. Wyeth painted a wonderfully atmospheric portrait of a dandified Hickok unmasking a card cheat in typical form. But his tenure in the cow town came to a disastrous end when he accidentally shot and killed his deputy,

Mike Williams, during a gunfight with gambler Phil Coe. Hickok was devastated by Williams's death, weeping copiously as he laid the body on a snooker table in the saloon. Hickok paid for the deputy's funeral. After eight months of Hickok's cleanup Abilene Town Council decided not to renew his expensive contract, and decided to ban the cattle drives instead.

Jobless, Hickok drifted east. In 1873 he joined Buffalo Bill Cody and Texas Jack Omohundro in their *"Scouts of the Plains"* revue. But Bill hated the work and was hopeless in his starring role. By this time he was an unsteady drunk and had a surprisingly high, girlish voice that left him open to ridicule. Drink had also left him ill-tempered, and he often threatened to shoot the stagehands. He left the show, and in March 1876 he married fifty-year-old circus proprietor Agnes Thatcher Lake. A few months later he joined his friend Charlie Utter in a trek to the goldfields of South Dakota. They arrived in Deadwood, Dakota Territory, in July 1876. Hickok seems to have had a premonition that he would meet his end in the town and wrote to his wife, "Agnes darling, if such should be we never meet again, while firing my last shot, I will gently breathe the name of my wife – Agnes – and with wishes even for my enemies I will make the plunge and try to swim to the other shore."

The end arrived on August 2, 1876, as Hickok played poker in Nuttal & Mann's Saloon. Unable to take his usual seat with its back to the wall, Hickok twice asked fellow player Charles Rich to swap with him, but to no avail. By this stage in his life Hickok's eyesight was failing, due to trachoma, so he was particularly concerned for his safety. As he played, a cowardly ex-buffalo hunter, Jack McCall, walked within a few feet of Hickok, shouted "Take that!" and shot the ageing gunfighter in the back of the head. As he fell, his hand of cards scattered on the table; the ace of spades, ace of clubs, eight of clubs, eight of spades, and queen or jack of diamonds. The hand is known to this day as the "Dead man's hand."

Hickok's contemporary obituary in the *Cheyenne Daily Leader* was scathing. It implied that he was an obsolete figure from the "lawless times" of the past, who had degenerated into a "tame and worthless loafer," his constitution ruined by "wine and women." But his Deadwood grave is visited to this day, and his legend is undiminished. Any gunman would have done well to listen to his professional advice, given in an interview of 1865, "Take time. I've known many a feller slip up for shootin' in a hurry." He maintained that he valued accuracy rather than speed, but then he was one of the fastest draws ever known in the West.

Hickok's friend Charlie Utter placed a death notice for his friend in the *Black Hills Pioneer,* "Died in Deadwood, Black Hills, August 2, 1876, from the effects of a

pistol shot, J.B. Hickock [sic] (Wild Bill) formerly of Cheyenne, Wyoming. Funeral services will be held at Charlie Utter's Camp, on Thursday afternoon, August 3, 1876." Almost the entire town attended the funeral. Hickok's grave in Deadwood's Ingleside Cemetery was identified with a wooden marker, on which was written "Pard, we will meet in the happy hunting ground to part no more. Good bye, Colorado Charlie, C. H. Utter."

Perhaps of all of the Western gunfighters, Hickok was the closest to the stereotype: a ruthless and prolific killer, dueller, law man, and gambler who never had a quiet day in his life.

Above: A photograph of the cast of Cody's 1873 show, *"The Scouts of the Plains"*. Hickok is second from the left, seated next to Texas Jack.

Left: N.C. Wyeth's moody portrait of Wild Bill Hickok unmasking a chard cheat. Wyeth enjoyed painting the mercurial Hickok.

Below: Hickok's tombstone bears Charley Utter's moving epitaph. Sadly, his name is misspelled.

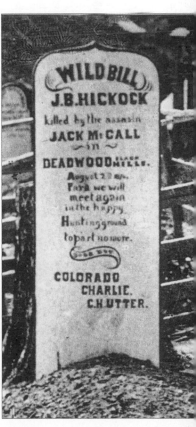

Doc Holliday

John "Doc" Holliday was unusual amongst the gunfighters, good and bad, in that he came from a well-to-do background. He was born on August 14, 1851, in Griffin, Georgia, to Henry Burroughs Holliday and Alice Jane Holliday. He was their eldest surviving child. Henry Holliday was a Confederate major in the Civil War, and was later elected Major of Valdosa, Georgia. But misfortune came early in his life. John was intensely close to his mother, Alice, but she died in 1866. To compound his loss, his father remarried within an indecently hasty three months.

Equally atypical for a Western gunman, Holliday studied for a university degree. He qualified as a doctor in dental surgery in Philadelphia. But a second major blow

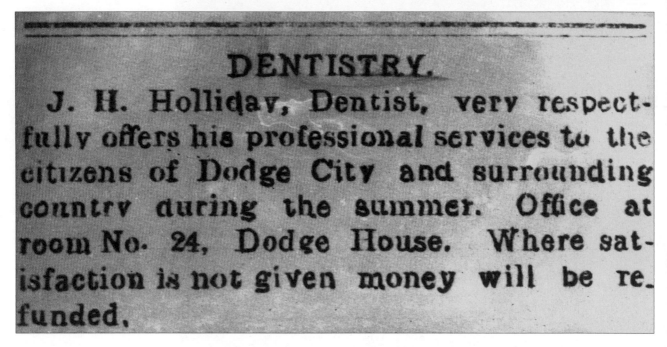

DENTISTRY.

J. H. Holliday, Dentist, very respectfully offers his professional services to the citizens of Dodge City and surrounding country during the summer. Office at room No. 24, Dodge House. Where satisfaction is not given money will be refunded.

Above: Holliday began his professional life as a dentist, but decided to pursue an alternative career as a gambler and gunman.

was to befall him soon after his graduation, when he was diagnosed with tuberculosis. Effectively, he spent the balance of his life on borrowed time, and this may have accounted for the extremely cavalier way he led it.

Holliday began to practice dentistry in various Western boomtowns, including Dodge City, but his illness necessitated a move west to a hotter, drier climate. By now he was too ill to follow his profession, so he headed west to Dallas and, like so many men of his type, he became a professional gambler. Fellow gunman and sometimes friend Bat Masterson described Doc as being of a "mean disposition and an

ungovernable temper, and under the influence of liquor (he) was a most dangerous man." His unpleasant temper and vagabond lifestyle was to descend into a corrosive cocktail of violence and murder. Holliday went about armed with a gun in a shoulder holster, a gun on his hip and a long, wicked knife. His long list of killings started with the murder of a local gambler in Dallas, and a pattern of "kill and run" established itself. Doc was never again to feel safe in one place for too long. The most foolish murder he committed was that of a soldier from Fort Richardson, which brought him to the attention of the United States Government. Doc escaped,

Above: A gunfighter's Heiser shoulder holster.

Above: Big Nose Kate had a volatile relationship with Doc Holliday.

but now had a price on his head and was wanted by the law. He moved to Denver, and managed to remain anonymous until his violent temper re-surfaced. He slashed a gambler, Bud Ryan, with his long knife, and almost killed him. At this time, he also became involved with the only woman that stayed in his life for any length of time, the infamously named "Big Nose" Kate. Big Nose was a well-known madam and prostitute, reputed to practice these professions through choice. She was also one of the most famous of the gunwomen of the West, and an excellent shot. Although she and Doc attempted to live together respectably, the bright saloon lights were her natural habitat and she returned to them time after time. Their relationship lasted, on and off, for many years, but it was always highly volatile. On one occasion, Big Nose sprang Doc from jail in Fort Griffin, but when their relationship soured, she just as quickly turned him in. The pattern of Doc's life was now set. Effectively, he was a professional killer. He rode with Wyatt Earp for some time, using the opportunity to add to his murder tally. One of Holliday's few redeeming features was his deep sense of loyalty to his friends and to Earp in particular. Earp described him as a "most skilful gambler, and the nerviest, fastest, deadliest man with a six-gun I ever saw." But although Wyatt valued Holliday, he was also embarrassed by his terrible, violent behavior.

Although Doc claimed he had escaped nine attempts on his life (five ambushes and four hangings), he finally died in bed in Glenwood Springs, Colorado. His failing health had led him to this health resort, to try the sulphur spring water. He was just thirty-six years old, but contemporary accounts described his body as being so ravaged by drink and illness that he looked like a man of eighty. At the end, he took to his bed for fifty-seven days, and was delirious for fourteen of them. Considering his style of life, this was a very strange way for him to die. His final words probably referred to this: "This is funny," he said.

Jesse James

Jesse James was born in Clay County, Missouri, on September 5, 1847. He was four years younger than his brother Frank James, but Jesse was to dominate Frank throughout his life. Jesse fought notionally on the Confederate side during the Civil War, but was actually embroiled in a parallel guerrilla campaign waged by various sets of bushwhackers, including the Quantrill gang. Their activities mainly consisted of raiding, stealing, and murdering civilians. Jesse's commanding officer noted

Below: An early photograph of Jesse Woodson James. His gang invented the bank robbery and initiated a sixteen-year-long murder spree.

that he was the "keenest...fighter in the command." Frank James was a member of the secessionist Drew Lobbs Army, whose violent activities led to the family being expelled from Clay County. This period in Jesse's life formed his outlook for life. His father, Robert James (a Baptist minister), had been murdered by Kansas raiders, and his formidable mother, Zerelda James Samuel, was imprisoned for spying against the Union. He himself had been badly wounded in the chest during a shootout with a party of Union cavalry. This all led to an enduring hatred of everything that reminded him of the "oppressive" North, including banks and trains.

When he returned home from the war, Jesse formed a family gang of outlaws together with his brother Frank and four younger half-brothers. At first, as they confined their attacks to the aforementioned banks and trains, the James gang had some public support. They are also credited with having perpetrated the first armed bank robbery in United States history, raiding the Clay County Savings Association in Liberty, Missouri, in February 1866. Unfortunately, an innocent schoolboy was killed as they made their escape. Despite this, John Newman Edwards, the famous Missouri editor, referred to Jesse as "America's Robin Hood" who had a "chivalry of crime." Perhaps James's most enduring claim to fame is that he and his gang invented the bank robbery and staged the first large-scale train hold-up in the country's history.

Left: N.C. Wyeth's shadowy portrait of the James gang in hiding conveys a sense of weary watchfulness and high tension. Jesse has the haunted look of a wanted man.

Merwin Hulbert Revolvers

Merwin Hulbert and Co. were New York dealers, promoters, and marketers of firearms. They made no weapons themselves but instead contracted with other manufacturers to supply them with guns, usually under their own brand. This 1880s range of neat, compact center-fire revolvers was made for them by Hopkins and Allen, and came in a number of styles. All used an unusual loading

One of these guns is known to have been owned by Jesse James in 1882, the year he was murdered.

SPECIFICATIONS

Type: six-shot single-action revolver

Origin: Hopkins and Allen, Norwich, Connecticut

Caliber: .44-40

Barrel Length: 3¼in-7 inches

mechanism, where the barrel and cylinder assembly were twisted sideways then pulled forward to allow the cartridge cases to drop out and new rounds to be inserted. One of the early Hulbert/ Hopkins and Allen pocket (First and Second models), the single-action weapon

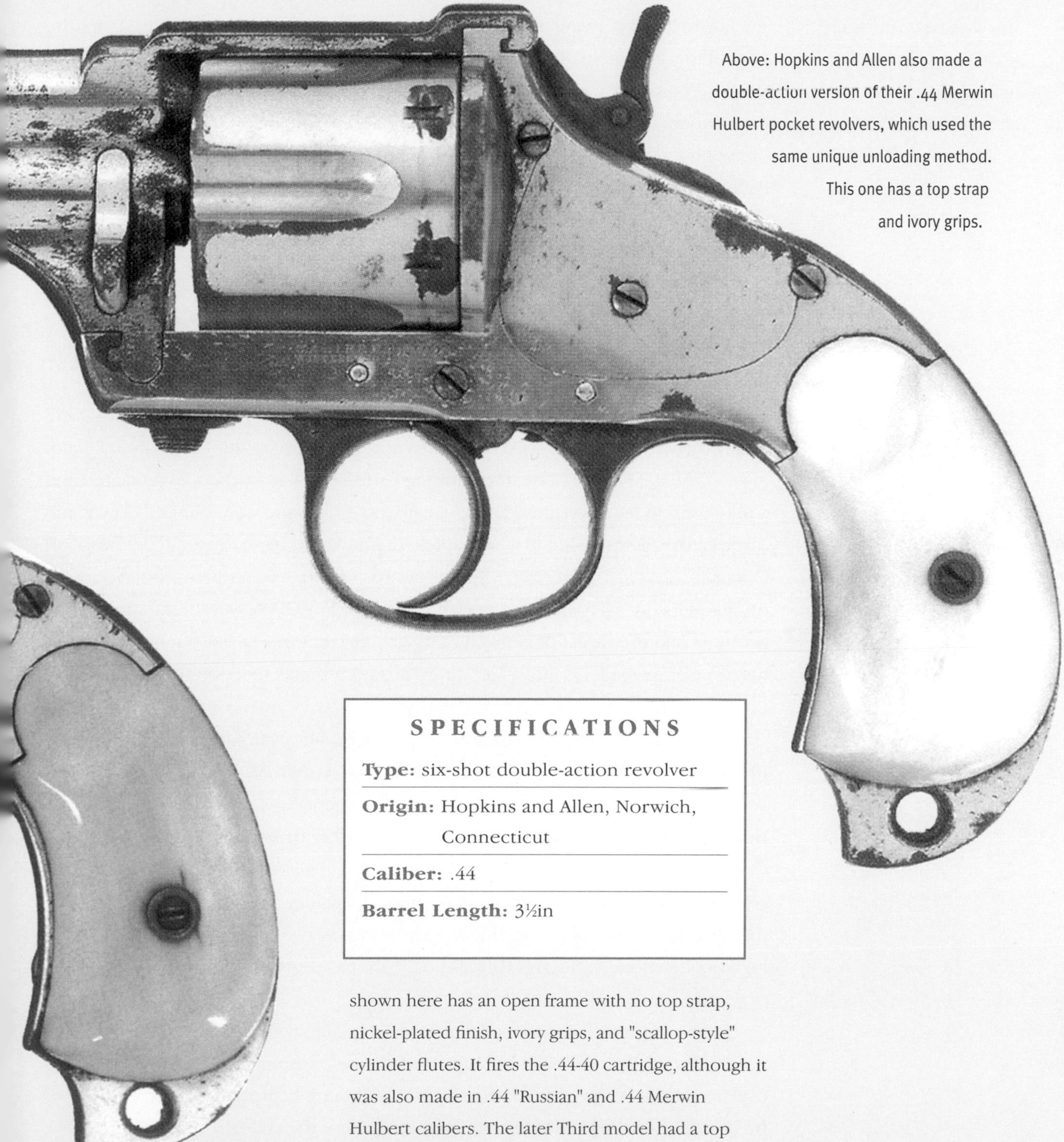

Above: Hopkins and Allen also made a double-action version of their .44 Merwin Hulbert pocket revolvers, which used the same unique unloading method. This one has a top strap and ivory grips.

SPECIFICATIONS

Type: six-shot double-action revolver

Origin: Hopkins and Allen, Norwich, Connecticut

Caliber: .44

Barrel Length: 3½in

shown here has an open frame with no top strap, nickel-plated finish, ivory grips, and "scallop-style" cylinder flutes. It fires the .44-40 cartridge, although it was also made in .44 "Russian" and .44 Merwin Hulbert calibers. The later Third model had a top strap and more conventional flutes.

Opposite page: Frank and Jesse James pose with the tools of the trade shortly after the Civil War.

James played along with his press image, handing a press release to the conductor of a train that the gang had just raided. It helpfully described their attack as the "Most Daring Robbery on Record." He considerately left blanks for the newspapers to fill in with the value of their spoils. Finally, the banks grew tired of the gang's activities and brought in the Pinkerton Detective Agency. Despite the Pinks' famous motto, "We Never Sleep," the gang successfully gunned down several agents who tried to infiltrate their home territory. Frustration finally led the Agency to mount a grenade attack on the James family home in 1875. This backfired disastrously. Frank and Jesse's nine-year-old half-brother was killed in the raid and their mother's arm was so badly shattered that it had to be amputated. The Agency was roundly condemned for this barbaric behavior, and the James Gang were very nearly awarded an amnesty.

The gang continued their spree of thieving and murder until the tables were finally turned on them in 1876. They attempted to hold up the First National Bank in Northfield, Minnesota, but the bank staff and several townspeople retaliated and a massive gun battle ensued. Three members of the gang were gunned down, and three of the James brothers were captured. Frank and Jesse escaped, but Missouri Governor Thomas Crittenden offered rewards of $10,000 (reputedly on the advice of Allan Pinkerton) for turning in either Jesse or Frank. Pressure tightened on the brothers and the threat of betrayal hung around their necks like a millstone. Jesse hardly ever took off his guns, and never turned his back to a door or window if he could help it.

Ultimately, the massive reward led to Jesse's betrayal. James Gang members Robert and Charley Ford gunned him down in his own St. Joseph home. He had very unwisely put down his gun, just for a moment, to adjust a crooked picture. But the Fords were forced to share the reward with several officials, including Crittenden, and were shunned and ridiculed as back-shooting cowards. Charley couldn't stand this treatment and committed suicide. Robert was condemned to the even worse fate of re-enacting the shooting every night in a stage show, where he was often booed off stage. He was finally shot to death in a tent saloon in Creede, Colorado.

Jesse's ruthless campaign of murder and pillage, which had lasted for sixteen years, was finally over. His death concluded one of the most serious crime waves ever to hit the West. Jesse's rather bizarre and fiercely protective mother insisted he be buried in the yard of the family home, where she charged visitors twenty-five cents each to see his tombstone, which read:

Right: A collection of weaponry and equipment owned by The Outlaws.

Jesse W James
Died 3 April 1882
Aged 34 years, 6 months, 28 days
Murdered by a traitor and a coward
whose name is not worthy
to appear here.

Frank James couldn't take any more of the claustrophobic outlaw life without his brother to boss him around.

He turned himself in, saying, "I am tired of this life of taut nerves, of night-riding, and day-hiding... tired of seeing Judas on the face of every friend I know." N.C. Wyeth brought this paranoiac tension to life in his portrait of the James gang in hiding: anxiety is etched into each face; each man nervously clutches his gun. A strangely sympathetic Missouri jury refused to convict Frank, and he gave up his life of crime, spending the remainder of his life in various humdrum jobs.

Even during their lifetime, the James gang were the subject of many dime novels, but their personality cult really took off after Jesse's death. There were many postmortem sightings of him, just as there would be for Elvis in the twentieth century. But his death also signalled the fact that the "era of the bad man" was drawing to a close. Better methods of law enforcement meant that outlaws felt more and more exposed and were forced to hide in more and more remote regions to escape detection.

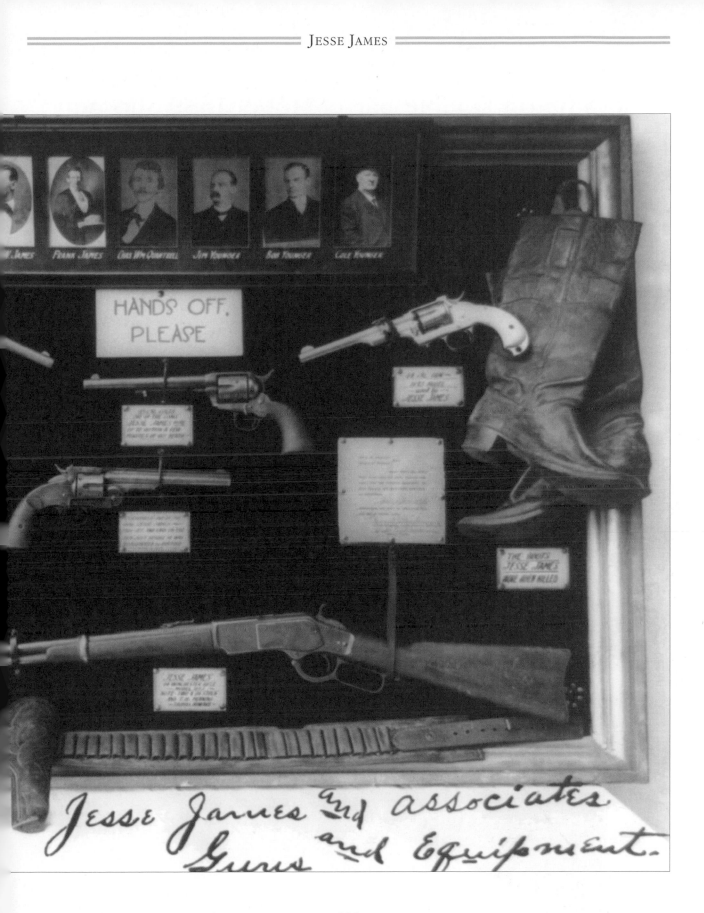

Remington Double Barrel Model 1889 Shotgun

By the 1880s we start to see a new character on the scene. His respectable dress sets him apart from the cowhands. These were professional men like the famous Doc Holliday, a qualified dentist. As a respected member of the community, Holliday became a member of Wyatt Earp's Dodge City Peace Commission. His weapon of choice was usually a shotgun, and Earp described him as "the nerviest, fastest, deadliest man with a six-gun I ever saw." He was also a professional gambler and killer, a sinister and surprising combination in a medical man. I am sure we would find the Doc in a Dodge City alleyway holding several bad guys "backed against the wall," courtesy of his shotgun.

Above: Close-up of the checkered pistol grip and double triggers show that the gun has been well-used.

Below: The barrels have been shortened to give a devastating blast at close range.

SPECIFICATIONS

Caliber: 12 gauge

Length of barrel: 18 inches

Barrel shape: Round

Finish: Browned steel

Grips: Walnut, checkered with pistol grip

Action: Breech loading double barrel

Year of manufacture: 1889

Manufacturer: Remington Arms Company, Ilion, New York

Western Shotguns were specially designed to create respect in close quarter fights. They had shortened barrels to allow for maneuverability and a widespread shot pattern. To this day, criminals saw off gun barrels to achieve the same effect. At close range, a twitch in the Doc's fingers would send the bad guys "all to hell in pieces." The Remington shown here has a pistol grip stock to allow the gun to be fired from the hip and external hammers for quick cocking. This type of gun was particularly popular with law enforcement agents and stagecoach guards.

Colt Model 1860 Army Revolver

Below: Detail of the cylinder and hammer.
The frame screws have seen better days!

SPECIFICATIONS

Caliber: 0.44

Length of barrel: 8 inches

Barrel shape: Round

Finish: Gray patina

Grips: Walnut

Action: Single

Year of manufacture: 1860

Manufacturer: Samuel Colt,
   Hartford, Connecticut

When the Civil War began, Samuel Colt was anxious to support the Union forces despite having made pre-war sales worth around three million dollars to the South. His plans for his own special division, Colts Rifles, which would have operated outside state control, were thwarted. But it was recognized that his ability to produce some of the finest firearms then available was a major asset to the Union cause.

Left: In many ways, a nicer-looking gun than its tremendously successful replacement, the Peacemaker.

Above: The rounded barrel section and cutaway in front of the cylinder distinguish this gun from its sister arm – the Navy.

When Colt replaced the Dragoon model in 1860, he was determined to correct one of that model's major disadvantages, its weight. The earlier gun weighed a full four pounds, two ounces, whilst his later version weighed in at a more manageable two pounds, ten ounces. The new gun was produced between 1860 and 1873, when it was finally replaced by the Peacemaker. Over 200,000 examples were manufactured. The Union government purchased 120,000 of these to supply their troops during the Civil War. The result was that many of these weapons were still in circulation on the frontier in the 1870's. In fact, it is likely that vaunted lawman Wyatt Earp carried one of these weapons, rather than the Buntline Special that legend has

decreed. The gun itself is probably one of the most familiar-looking Colts ever made, and has rather elegant proportions. A streamlined cylinder and a long, slim barrel make it less chunky-looking than the Single Action model that replaced it.

Our featured weapon is a composite model, meaning that it has different serial numbers on the frame, barrel, wedge, and cylinder, showing that these parts have been interchanged at some time in its history. Presumably, this was during its military life. The original factory die-rolled scene of a Mexican War naval engagement is clearly visible on the cylinder.

Bat Masterson

Above: William Barclay Masterson, a leading member of the Dodge City Gang. He was always sartorially elegant.

Bat Masterson was undoubtedly one of the most colorful characters of the Old West. "Gentleman Lawman," dandy, gunfighter, and notorious gambler, his profile is archetypal of the Western gunman.

Bat was born Bartholomew Masterson in November 1853 (sometime between the 23rd and 26th) in Quebec, Canada, the son of a prairie farmer. He would later change his name to William Barclay Masterson, but became known at "Bat" after the "batting" walking cane he would carry later in his life. He was one of five notorious brothers born to Thomas and Catherine Masterson, who farmed in both Canada and the United States. The brothers (George, Thomas, Edward J., Bat, and James) went on to become famous in the area of law enforcement, and especially for bringing the infamous Dodge City under the rule of law. The family moved to Sedgwick County, Kansas, in 1871, where several of the Masterson brothers drifted away from the life of the farm to try their hand at buffalo hunting. Neither Bat nor his brother Ed were very interested in pursuing an education, so they took jobs as railroad graders for the Atchison, Topeka, and Santa Fe Railroad. The job took the brothers to Dodge City for the first time, working for contractor Raymond Ritter. But when Ritter skipped town owing the brothers $300, Bat and Ed moved on to a more glamorous life as buffalo hunters, supplying meat to the railroad crews they had worked with. In 1872, Bat first came into contact with Wyatt Earp while both young men were hunting buffalo on the Salt Fork of the Arkansas, and a lifelong friendship began.

Based in the panhandle town of Adobe Walls, Texas, Bat was soon to come into contact with Quanah Parker's Comanche and Cheyenne braves when the disgruntled Indians attacked the town on June 27, 1874. Effectively, the Plains tribes were being starved out of their traditional way of life by the decimation of the buffalo by professional hunters like the Masterson brothers. The white hunters, armed with their "Big Fifty" Sharps rifles, were gradually pushing the vast plains herds to the verge of extinction. At the age of twenty, Bat was the town's youngest defender at the "Battle of Adobe Walls." This was his first taste of real fighting. Five hundred Indians attacked around thirty-five settlers, but luckily the town consisted mostly of sod houses, which were impervious to the Indians' arrows. After an attack that lasted several hours, in which four settlers were killed and around thirty Indians fell, the tribes withdrew. The United States Army then deployed men from Fort Leavenworth to relieve the beleaguered defenders of Adobe Walls, fighting under the command of General Nelson A. Mills. The army hired Bat and his friend Billy Dixon as scouts, and they rode with them during the Texas panhandle campaign. For the rest of the early 1870s Bat drifted through Colorado, Kansas, Texas, Arizona, and other locations, hunting and scouting.

The next milestone in Bat's career happened in 1876 when Bat shot and killed his first man in a gunfight in Sweetwater, Texas. Bat had become involved with local girl Molly Brennan. When her former lover, Sgt. Melvin King, caught them together in the saloon, he drew on the pair. Molly interposed herself to save Masterson and was shot dead for her loyalty. The bullet that killed Molly lodged itself in Bat's hip and disabled him for life, leaving him with a pronounced limp. Masterson then gunned down King, who died the next day.

This cool and calculated barroom brawling in the company of prostitutes was to set the scene for much of Bat's middle life. In the summer of 1876, Bat was drawn back to the notorious Dodge City. At this time, his brother George was bartender of the premier dance hall and saloon in the town, Varieties, and his friend Wyatt Earp was town Marshal. Bat worked as Earp's deputy, patrolling Front Street for several weeks, swinging his walking cane. He left in July to follow the gold rush to Deadwood, but only got as far as Cheyenne, Wyoming, where he worked the gambling trade as a faro banker. In spring 1877, Masterson returned to Dodge for the cattle season. Dodge City had been founded on the Santa Fe Trail, close to Fort

Above: Comanche chief Quanah Parker with his wife Tonasa in 1892. They are standing on the porch of their five-bedroom house.

Above: A rattlesnake
skin necktie.

Dodge, alongside the Atchison, Topeka, and Santa Fe Railroad. The town had first been populated by buffalo hunters and gradually attracted a rough merchant class, whose business was shipping buffalo hides east. By 1873 the town was already known as a focus of crime, with no organized law, and became known at the "Wickedest City in America." In fact, the town became so violent that its cemetery, Boot Hill, was one of the best-known local landmarks.

A handsome dandy, Bat now joined his brothers Ed and James ("Jim") in this volatile town. Jim was the co-owner of a Dodge City saloon and dancehall, while Ed (the eldest Masterson brother) was assistant marshal to Marshal Larry Deger. Deger and Bat soon came to blows when Bat appeared to be drunk and disorderly, and their relationship worsened when Bat aided and abetted the criminal Bobby Gill to skip town. Both men were thrown into jail and fined for their misdemeanors. Gill was given a railroad ticket to leave Dodge City, but Bat remained. Bat subsequently became a peripheral member of the Dodge City Gang. This was a group of local "businessmen" that consisted mostly of renegade Indian fighters and teamsters. They were eager to exploit Dodge City's loose morals to make themselves rich, and were against excessive law enforcement. When Deger arrested gambler and gang sympathizer Charlie Ronan, gang leader Major James "Dog" Kelley invited Bat Masterson to arrest his boss, along with fellow lawman Joe Mason. This resulted in a bizarre situation where both the town's mayor and marshal ended up in prison.

By this time Bat was a well-known figure in the town. His dark hair and blue eyes, coupled with his conspicuous style of dress (which included a sombrero with a snakeskin hat band, red silk neck scarf, gold spurs, and silver-plated six-shooters) led to him being instantly recognizable. He bought a share in Dodge's Lone Star dance hall, and became part of the town hierarchy. This helped him to be elected county sheriff in November 1877, beating Deger by three votes. Now a fully-fledged lawman at the age of twenty-four, he traded his slightly eccentric ensemble for the tailor-made black suit, bowler hat, and walking cane that were to become his trademark apparel. He appointed Charlie Bassett as his undersheriff and began to tame the town. Ed Masterson also became town Marshal in place of Deger, so that the two Masterson brothers controlled the law not only in Dodge City but in all of Ford County.

Below: Lawrence E. Deger, marshal of Dodge City. He became mayor of the town in 1883.

Just a month after his appointment, a six-man gang of outlaws held up a train in the next county. Bat led a posse that captured two members of the gang without firing a shot. He and his brother Ed captured two more of the gang as they approached Dodge City itself, again without a fight. Despite this restraint, Bat's reputation as a gunfighter helped to put down the inevitable saloon brawls and general lawlessness in Dodge. Many criminals chose to avoid the town, rather than face its gun-toting sheriff. But sadly, Bat was unable to prevent a gunfight between his brother, Deputy Marshal Ed Masterson, and two drunken cowboys in which Ed was gunned down and killed. Never a gunfighter in the same league as Bat, poor Ed had practiced his gun skills by shooting cans off fences, but his draw was too slow to save him. He was buried in the cemetery at Fort Dodge. Bat is said to have shot both men in revenge for his brother's death, killing one and maiming the other. After Ed's death in April 1878, Bat hired his brother Jim as his deputy, cracked down on the use of guns in Dodge, and enforced a 9 p.m. curfew. In January of the following year (1879), Bat was appointed U.S. deputy marshall for the region. At this time, a "turf war" had broken out between two local railroad companies (the Denver and Rio Grande, and the Atchison, Topeka, and Santa Fe), who both wanted to build the line to Deadwood. Bat was obliged to protect the workers of both companies from being killed or injured in shootouts between rival workers. Despite

his effectiveness, Bat lost his campaign for re-election in November 1879, and Jim Masterson was elected town marshal in his place, at a reduced salary of $50 a month. Bat's defeat can probably be attributed to the fact that many Dodge City residents were sick of the influence of the Dodge City Gang and longed for a more peaceful way of life in a town that was not run for the benefit of the saloon owners.

Even at this time, there was a general disaffection with the "frontier characters" of Dodge and their gun-slinging ways, and their "flitting" to other towns was welcome to many.

Left: Dodge City's famous Long Branch Saloon. Built in the late 1870's, Luke Short bought a partial interest in the business in 1883. It was the scene of countless shootings, gunfights, and standoffs.

Unabashed, Bat made his living from the law and gambling (mostly playing faro) for the next few years. He drifted to the boomtown of Leadville, Colorado. By early 1881, he had made it as far as another iconic Western town: Tombstone, Arizona. Here he continued his close friendship with Wyatt Earp, who was the proprietor of the Oriental Saloon in the town. Bat is credited with introducing Earp to drinking and faro, and spent many nights in the Oriental, gambling with poker pals Doc Holliday, Wyatt Earp, and Luke Short. Ironically, Bat was to the leave Tombstone just before the O.K. Corral "incident," returning to Dodge City to support his brother Jim. Jim Masterson had become partners with A.J. Peacock in Dodge's Lady Gay saloon, but had fallen out with both Peacock and Peacock's brother-in-law, Al Updegraff, who had been working there as a bartender. As soon as Bat arrived in Dodge by train at noon on April 16, 1881, a shootout began between Peacock and Updegraff, the Masterson brothers, and Charlie Ronan. The Fort Collins Courier of May 5, 1881, reported how Masterson shot Updegraff through the lung and fatally wounded him. In fact, this is completely inaccurate. Updegraff survived for a further two years until he died of smallpox. Despite the fact that he had almost certainly been fired on first, many townsfolk were disappointed by Bat's involvement in the firefight. The paper reported that "the good opinion many citizens had of Bat has been changed to one of contempt. The parties engaged in this reckless affray were permitted to leave town, though warrants were sworn out for their arrest… there is good reason to believe they will never darken Dodge City any more. " Amazingly, given his reputation, this is Bat's final recorded gunfight at the age of just twenty-seven. He was out of Dodge by nightfall.

In April 1882, Bat became the marshal of Trinidad, Colorado, and remained in the town for a year. But in 1883 he returned to Dodge City to support his friend and fellow Dodge City Gang member Luke Short in the so-called Dodge City War. Short had bought a half share in Dodge's Long Branch Saloon, but the town's Mayor, Alonzo B. Webster, was determined to drive men like Short out of business. Although he had won the 1881 election on the ticket of reforming the town, Webster himself was a saloon owner, and involved in the whiskey trade. Having fired Jim Masterson as city marshal, Webster instructed his own man, Sheriff Louis C. Hartman, to arrest several prostitutes that were working in Short's establishment. Short went to the town jail to try to get them released, and became involved in a shootout with Hartman. Luckily, Hartman was unharmed, but Short was kicked out of town. Outraged by the treatment he had received, Short called on all his old gunslinger friends to come to Dodge to support him. Bat Masterson, Wyatt Earp, Charlie Bassett, Frank McLain, Neal Brown, W.H. Harris, and W.F. Petillon all subsequently appeared to show their solidarity. Terrified by the assembled posse of well-known gunfighters and hard men, Webster negotiated with the level-headed Wyatt Earp to allow Luke Short to return to Dodge City and resume his business at the Long Branch. In fact, despite the potential for violence from the Commission, no one was killed in this stand-off. The most lasting souvenir of the event was the famous double-row photograph of the eight commission

members, taken by C.S. Fly in June 1883. Bat stands at the back, second from the right, easily identified by his trademark bowler hat and well-groomed moustache.

Over the next few years, Bat roamed the boom towns and cow towns of the Old West, including Dodge City, Denver, Trinidad, Reno, and Las Vegas. He gambled, promoted boxing matches, wrote a weekly sports column for a Denver paper, and became a theater producer. True to form, Bat initially ran a faro layout in the Arcade in Denver. Later, he bought the town's Palace Variety Theater, and in 1891, he married local actress Emma Walters. He also established the Olympic Athletic Club to promote boxing in the town. In 1896, Bat staged a boxing match to determine the new heavyweight champion. It was due to be held in El Paso, but when the Texas Rangers were sent in to break up the fight, Bat moved the action to Langtry. The huge purse of $10,000 was won by prizefighter Bob Fitzsimmons. Having staged the fight and protected the prize money, Bat then returned to Denver to write about the bout.

Above: Faro was a popular Western game of chance, played by many famous gunfighters, including Bat Masterson.

Throughout this period Bat remained an upholder of the law, as he swaggered about with his pair of pistols on prominent display. It certainly kept him out of trouble. In one form or another, Bat relied on his gunmanship throughout his adult life. In 1930, Arthur Chapman, writing in the New York Herald-Tribune, explained how Masterson perfected his skills "It was not magic which enabled Bat Masterson to produce some wizard-like effects with the draw. It was hard and unrelenting practice." Evidently, the young Bat and his roommate, "Conk" Jones, practiced gunplay for at least an hour each day, using unloaded pistols to endlessly "draw and click… draw and click" to improve the speed of their draw. Evidently, Masterson developed a strange way of "holstering" his gun, tying it to a string hung around his neck. But this is actually most unlikely. His gun of choice was the .45 caliber Colt revolver, which weighed around three pounds when loaded. Conk and Bat had a brief fallout later in their career, when Conk felt that his friend had taken advantage of a young and unwary poker player. Words were exchanged, but the pair had too much mutual respect to risk exchanging lead. Ultimately, Bat achieved the status of "Doctor of the Draw", and could back his actions with the unspoken threat of his gunmanship. But like many other western gunfighters, Masterson's reputation as a killer was greatly inflated. He was credited with over twenty-seven fatal shootings, but had actually killed only two or three men. His view of gun fighting was nothing if not succinct: "Always shoot first, and never miss."

As the nineteenth century drew to its close, many men of Bat's kind turned to drink and became troublesome to their neighbors. In 1898 there were reports that he, Wyatt Earp, Doc Holliday, Ed Casey, and Doc Brown of Spokane were on their way to Havana to introduce gambling to the island and establish a kind of southern "Monte Carlo." Few welcomed the prospect. Meanwhile, Bat became the victim of a vendetta by Otto Floto, the sports editor of the *Denver Post*. They had been in partnership to promote boxing matches but the relationship had soured. Ultimately, their antagonism resulted in a street brawl in July 1900. Masterson whipped Floto with his walking cane' and the infuriated newspaperman hired a gunman to avenge his humiliation, "Whispering" Jim Smith. Ultimately, Bat was forced to leave the city to avoid further trouble. Bat drifted east to New York, and became a sports writer for the *New York Morning Telegraph*. But he didn't stay out of trouble for long. In 1902, he was arrested and fined for running a crooked faro game in which George H. Snow (the son of the late president of the Mormon Church) lost the then-enormous sum of $16,000. Despite his gambling habit, Bat once more re-visited his career in law enforcement in 1905, when President Theodore Roosevelt appointed him as United States Marshal of New York. On December 15, 1905 *The Elbert County Banner* reported that "Bat Masterson, well known in Denver and throughout the West as a dead shot with a big number of notches on his gun, is to be appointed to the secret service at the White House." Bat kept the job until the following year, when he resigned to pursue his more lucrative newspaper work. Perhaps he also realized that the day of the gunman was over, and moved on with the times. He recounted many of his earlier experiences in his column in *Human Life* magazine and told stories of his well known confederates, including Wyatt Earp and Doc Holliday. He also wrote about Dodge City itself, and described how "gambling was not only the principal, (but the) best-paying industry of the town."

Above: Bat Masterson attired in his trademark outfit of tailor-made black suit and bowler hat.

In his final years, Bat spent his time writing columns and visiting gyms. On the morning of October 25, 1921, Bat went to work as usual as the sports writer for the New York Morning Telegraph. Bat sat behind his newspaper desk and wrote the following words with his ink pen, "There are those who argue that everything breaks even in this dump of a world of ours. I supposed these ginks who argue that way hold that because the rich man gets ice in the summer and the poor man gets it in the winter, things are breaking even for both. Maybe so, but I'll swear that I can't see it that way…" These were the last words he ever wrote. He died of a heart attack at his desk, at the age of sixty-eight. The paper described him as a "former Western gunman and resident of Colorado." During his extensive writing career, Bat had churned out more than four million words. Known for his integrity, Masterson asserted that "a sports writer who is not willing to stand by his honest judgment ought to chuck his job and try something else." Masterson's columns were crudely written but full of challenging statements that packed a punch. Damon Runyon, writing about Bat in 1933, said that the former gunman had "no literary style, but he had plenty of moxie."

Winchester 1866 Carbine

Right: The 1866 Carbine was named the Yellow
Boy after its distinctive brass receiver.

Below: The familiar slot
in the side which re-
ceived bullets. Normal
loading was by thumbing
the shells in.

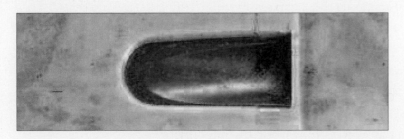

Although designed as a horseback weapon,
the Model 1866 Carbine also saw action in
the hands of gunfighters. Its compact
twenty-inch barrel, with no bolt action or
any other encumbrance, made it swift to
draw and just as easy to stow. It featured a
saddle ring on the left side of the frame for
extra security, and front and rear swivels
for carrying on a sling. The polished brass-

SPECIFICATIONS

Caliber: 0.44 rim fire
cartridge

Length of barrel: 20 inches

Barrel shape: Round

Finish: Blue Steel Barrel, brass
frame and receiver

Grips: Walnut

Action: Under lever repeating
with 14 shot magazine

Year of manufacture: 1866-91

Manufacturer: Winchester
Repeating Arms Company,
New Haven, Connecticut

alloy frame and receiver gave rise to its
nickname 'Yellow Boy'. The .44-inch rim
fire cartridge had its limitations when it
came to ultimate power, but this was more
than compensated for by its accuracy and

ease of use. With fourteen shots and a
quick reload action, you could put two
bullets into your intended target in the
time that it took to aim a higher-powered

single-shot rifle. This was tremendously useful for a wide range of targets including lawmen and guards. Jesse James used his Model 1866 to hold up trains and banks where the lighter carbine version would have doubtless proved a useful weapon.

Native Americans also aspired to Winchester ownership, as it put them one step ahead of their adversaries in the United States Cavalry. For the most part, cavalrymen were still using Civil War-issue, single-shot weapons. Indians acquired the weapons either by capturing them from settlers or buying them from unscrupulous white traders. Indian versions were often customized, with brass and nickel-plated studs hammered in to the stock and fore grip, together with rawhide tassels and beadwork. Many examples have survived.

Above: Left side view shows carbine ring. At $40 a time cowhands weren't about to lose this gun.

Texas Jack Omohundro

Opposite page: A dusty cattle herd being driven along the trail. Their average speed was ten to twelve miles a day.

"*My friends, perhaps many of you do not know this man whom we have gathered to honor. No doubt you would like to know something of him, who was one of my dearest and most intimate friends.*"

– Graveside tribute to Texas Jack by Buffalo Bill Cody

"*He was the Mustang King – The Conqueror of Cayuses without a rival. Horses came to him on the end of a lariat… He was a Knight in Silvered Sombrero, defender of women, subduer of bullies… He fought Comanches by the tribe and put them to death or flight. He led cavalry to the rescue of wagon trains. He saved officers' ladies from prairie fires… He had a heart so soft that it never failed the innocent and the friendless.*"

– *New York Times Magazine,* January 4, 1931

John Baker Omohundro was born on July 27, 1846. "Texas Jack's" family home was "Pleasure Hill" in Palmyra, Fluvanna County, Virginia. He was the fourth of John B. and Catherine Omohundro; "Baker" was his mother's maiden name. Buffalo Bill maintained that John was part Powhatan Indian and it is certainly true that he was a natural outdoorsman, scout, and tracker. He was reluctant to make the five-mile journey to school, preferring to fish, hunt, ride and shoot. As soon as he was old enough, he made his way to Texas to become a cowboy. Too young to fight when the Civil War broke out, he enlisted under General J.E.B. Stuart of the Confederate army as a courier and scout in 1861, and became known as the "Boy Scout of the Confederacy."

His elder brother Orville was a lieutenant in the Confederate Army. Ironically, some of John's best friends in later life were to be former Union soldiers. When the Civil War ended, Omohundro sailed to New Orleans and was subsequently shipwrecked on the west coast of Florida. Jack became a schoolteacher in Florida and then moved on to Texas on horseback. He became head of the Taylor ranch in Texas and returned to the cattle drives, negotiating the Chisholm Trail and driving cattle across Arkansas to beef-hungry Tennessee. The state was afflicted by drought and people were virtually starving, so they were extremely grateful for the cattle John drove into the area. This was how he earned his famous nickname. Buffalo Bill described this cattle-driving as tough work. "Life on the plains was a hardship and a trying duty," he noted. It wasn't only difficult, but dangerous. Cattle drivers

were often attacked by Indians, and on one occasion Jack lost seven of his cowboys. At around this time, Omohundro adopted a five-year-old boy who survived when his parents had been killed in an Indian attack by hiding under the floorboards of his pioneer home. Omohundro named him Texas Jack Jr. and taught him all he knew about cattle and horsemanship. Later, the boy was to work in Buffalo Bill's Wild West show with his adopted father and went on to be a showman in his own right, and to discover Will Rogers.

John continued on the cattle drives, and finally met Bill Cody in North Platte, Nebraska. Bill knew his reputation as an expert trailer and scout. They acted as guides for celebrities, including the Earl of Dunraven. Dunraven wrote about his experiences in Yellowstone and the Northwest in his memoirs, The Great Divide. He described Jack as "all life and blood and fire, blazing with suppressed poetry… a great personage." In 1872 they also guided a royal hunt with the Grand Duke Alexei Alexandrovich of Russia and several military men. In December that year, Cody and Omohundro met with dime novelist Ned Buntline. Buntline proposed that the three of them should bring a taste of their adventures on the western prairies to the stage. Buffalo Bill described how "he and I went East to go into the show business. He was the first to do a lasso act upon the stage." He described the opening night of *Scouts of the Prairie* as follows, "The Scouts of the Prairie was an Indian drama, of course, and there were between forty and fifty "supers" dressed as Indians. In the fight with them, Jack and I were at home. We blazed away at each other with blank cartridges, and when the scene ended in a hand-to-hand encounter, a general knock-down and drag-out, the way Jack and I killed Indians was a caution. We

Above: Grand Duke Alexis Alexandrovich of Russia, with puppy. The Grand Duke was the instigator of the famous royal hunt of 1872.

would kill them all off in one act, but they would come up again ready for business in the next. Finally, the curtain dropped, the play was ended, and I congratulated Jack and myself on having made such a brilliant and successful debut." *The Boston Journal* said of the pair, "Two finer specimens of manly strength and beauty were never seen on the stage or off the stage." The *Richmond Enquirer* said that "The way the Scouts handle their navy revolvers is the main secret of their success." Unlike other famous westerners that appeared on the show, Jack thoroughly enjoyed his acting career and his pleasant personality held the show together. Others, like Wild Bill Hickok, were much less enthusiastic about their stage antics. He lasted for only one season of the show, from 1873 to 1874, despite his friendship with the easygoing Omohundro. Cody had recruited Hickok to join the play in New York. Hickok had never been East, and was keen to see more of the States. Ultimately Omohundro and Cody paid him off with $500 each and a fine pistol, and Hickok returned to the West. Jack was also popular with the Indians who worked

Opposite page: Texas Jack Omohundro dressed to appear in Cody's show.

Opposite page: Cody's *Scouts of the Plains* show debuted in Chicago in 18972. It was produced by Ned Buntline.

on the show. They called him "White Chief" and the "Whirling Rope."

Scouts of the Prairie was immensely successful, and toured the country. When it reached Chicago, Jack met Josephine (or Giuseppina) Morlacchi, an Italian dancer and actress, who was playing the part of Dove Eye in the show. The pair continued to tour with the show together, strolling down the street, or dining together. They were married on September 1, 1873. The *Rochester Democrat and Chronicle* reported an announcement of their marriage: "The fair actress immediately took a liking to the gallant scout of the prairies, the renowned Indian fighter and buffalo hunter. The affection ripened, until it took the form of a declaration of love on the part of Omohundro, which resulted yesterday in a ceremony which made the twain one." The paper said that Josephine was originally from Milan, and that she was a highly educated, beautiful brunette. Jack himself was equally attractive, with an "aquiline nose, jet black hair, erect form, and piercing eye."

By 1877, Jack was running his own acting troupe, and like many great Western characters and "fighters", he wrote newspaper articles about his hunting and scouting experiences which were published in eastern newspapers and popular magazines.

Sadly, Jack's marriage to Josephine was only to last less than seven years. In 1880, Omohundro died of pneumonia at the tragic age of thirty-three. He was buried in the Evergreen Cemetery in Leadville, Colorado. Josephine was completely devastated and retired from the stage. She died of cancer only a few years later.

After his adoptive father's death, Texas Jack Jr. continued to tour the Wild West Show around the world. It was especially successful in South Africa. Bizarrely, Jack had another posthumous life, as a character in a series of highly-popular dime novels and newspaper articles written by several different Western writers, including Colonel Prentiss Ingraham and Joel Chandler Harris. He featured as a hero of the Confederacy. Herschel Logan published a famous biography of Jack in 1954, *Buckskin and Satin*.

Texas Jack is quite unusual among western gunmen. A brave and resourceful man who was handy with guns of all kinds, he never strayed onto to the wrong side of the law. On the contrary, he was a consummate gentleman, kind and loving, who took in orphans and faithfully loved his wife.

Omohundro was inducted into the Hall of Great Western Performers by National Cowboy Hall of Fame in Oklahoma City, Oklahoma. Sitting alongside such luminaries as John Wayne and Clint Eastwood, he is one of the few real cowboys among them.

Smith & Wesson Model No3

Below: Intricate engraving complements the S&W trademark in brass set into the walnut handgrip.

The .44 Russian was a more powerful version of the Smith & Wesson No. 3 revolver. The gun got its nomenclature through the company receiving a massive order for it from the Russian army. The order absorbed Smith & Wesson's entire manufacturing capacity for a full five years and almost brought the company to the verge of bankruptcy. The gun was manufactured around a special .44-inch internally-lubricated cartridge, specified by the Russian Army. This cartridge gave it excellent power and made the gun a serious rival to Colt's equivalent models of the 1870's. Revolvers manufactured for the Russian military order had an extra hump above the grip and a distinctive spur on the trigger guard.

The No. 3 Model remained in production for many years. This example has been engraved after leaving the factory. Embellishment of this kind was not unusual. The dark blue/black casehardened finish of the barrel cylinderand top-break frame contrasts beautifully with the engraving, which is filled in with gilt to set it off. It is both fancy and deadly.

A holstered brace of these revolvers was serious equipment for the western gunfighter.

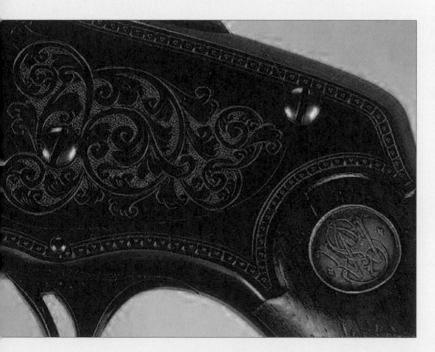

Right: The top break action allowed for the whole barrel and chamber assembly to hinge forward for reloading. Note the intricate carved pattern around the pivot pin.

Left: A Work of Art-the beautifully engineered .44 Russian revolver.

SPECIFICATIONS

Caliber: 0.44 Russian

Length of barrel: 6 inches

Barrel shape: Ribbed

Finish: Blue/black steel with gilt inlay engraving

Grips: Checkered walnut

Action: Single action revolver

Year of manufacture: from 1875

Manufacturer: Smith & Wesson, Springfield, Massachusetts

Commodore Perry Owens

Opposite page: John S. Fuller wrote a famous poem about Commodore Perry Owens, describing him as the "Law of the West."

Commodore Perry Owens (named for the famous naval commander) was a gunman who stood square on the side of law and order. But his methods were rooted in the style of the Old West, and soon got him into trouble.

Owens ran away from his Tennessee home at the age of thirteen. Teased for his unusual name, he cultivated a famously flamboyant appearance, with waist-length, strawberry-blonde hair and a neatly trimmed moustache. He started out as a roping and branding cowboy, but also worked as a buffalo hunter and for Wells Fargo. He was considered a dead shot, and became famous for his use of the cross-draw of the brace of pistols he wore around his hips. The technique gave him a split-second advantage over his opponents. For tough jobs, he also carried a Winchester.

While working as a cattle foreman, Owens got into trouble for shooting a Navajo horse rustler. He was tried for the offense, but acquitted. His notoriety helped him to get elected as the sheriff of Apache County, Arizona, where he was responsible for over 21,000 square miles of lawless territory. His reputation for iron nerves ad brilliant horsemanship preceded him. During his time in the job as a single-handed law enforcer, Owens tamed the volatile town of Holbrook, shooting six members of the Snider Gang in the notorious Round Valley Gunfight. He also became involved in the Pleasant Valley War. This was a turf feud between families of cattle ranchers and sheep farmers. Under pressure to serve an arrest warrant on the horse rustler Andy Blevins (who also used the alias of "Cooper"), Sheriff Owens went out to the Blevins family ranch. Unfortunately, Cooper refused to come quietly, and a shootout ensued. Within a minute, Owens had fired five shots, four of which killed Cooper, Sam Blevins, and Mose Roberts, and wounded John Blevins. Owens would probably have been hailed as a hero, except that Sam Blevins was little more than a boy (although he had been armed and ready to kill the lawman). Sam's death turned the tide of public opinion against Owens, and an inquest ensued. Although he was acquitted of any blameworthy conduct, the *Saint Johns Herald* distilled the general mood: "The common people are beginning to think that our territory has had enough of desperadoes as 'peace' officers… [who] shoot whom they please."

Aggrieved by this treatment, Owens scrawled this message on the back of Andy Cooper's tombstone: "Party against whom this warrant was issued was killed while resisting arrest." Owens was relieved of his commission, and the court officials attempted to withhold his outstanding pay until he took this from them at gunpoint.

Leaving his steady job, Owens became a gun for hire on the side of law enforcement. For a time, he worked as a guard for the Atlantic and Pacific Railroad, but later returned to public service as a Deputy U.S. Marshall.

William Clarke Quantrill

Above: A romantic portrait of William Clarke Quantrill.

Opposite page: A daguerreotype of Quantrill made when he was fifteen. Stories of his depravity were already circulating.

William Quantrill was one of the most infamous bad men of the post-Civil War period. Intelligent and good-looking, he was almost certainly a psychopath and a documented mass murderer. Unusually, he was also well-educated and a qualified teacher, but rejected his profession to live by the gun.

Born in Dover, Ohio on July 31, 1837, his parents were Caroline Cornelia Clarke and Thomas Quantrill. The Quantrills were "Free-Soil" Unionists, who believed that a slavery-free America would be a stronger and godlier country. William was the eldest of eight children. Even during his childhood years there were disturbing rumors of cruelty to animals and other children that would indicate that he was already a seriously disturbed individual. Despite this, Quantrill was well-educated, and began his adult life as a school teacher. For several years he taught school in Ohio, but in 1858 he travelled to Utah Territory with a Federal army wagon train. His ambition was to make more money than he had in his teaching job, and his role was to resupply the troops for their on-going fight against the Mormons. Quantrill decided to abandon his profession (at least temporarily), and assumed a completely new identity as Charles Hart, gambler and petty thief. He moved on to Lawrence, Kansas, in 1859 and taught school once more until 1860. By this time he was wanted for horse theft and murder (both capital offenses) and was forced to flee to Missouri. During his time in the South, it appears that Quantrill completely turned his back on his Unionist family background, becoming pro-Confederate and anti-abolitionist. When the Civil War began in 1861 he claimed to be a native of Maryland and enlisted on the Confederate side in the Missouri State Guard. But he soon became disenchanted with army discipline, and within months of joining up he had formed a band of guerilla troops known as Quantrill's Raiders. Their double aim was to be a thorn in the side of the Union and to become rich. At this stage he commanded no more than a dozen men, but they ambitiously robbed mail coaches and Union supply convoys, while attacking Unionist towns, troops, and civilians. Most of this activity took place along the Kansas-Missouri border and often involved

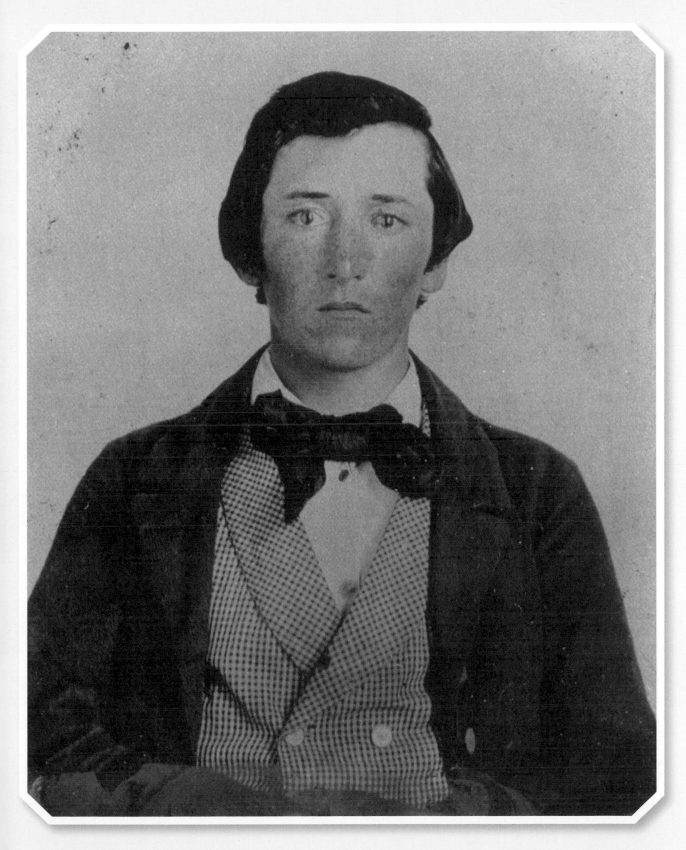

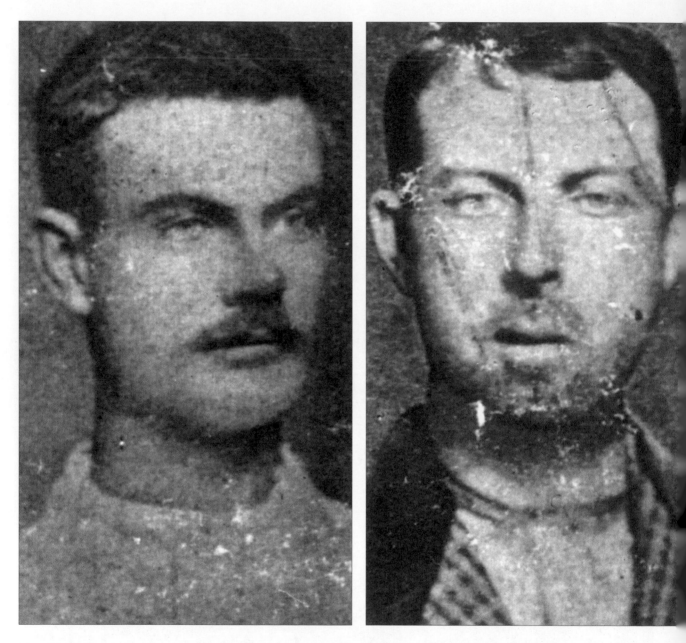

Above: James Younger (left) and Bob Younger (right). Both were captured at Northfield and jailed.

conflict with the so-called Jayhawkers. These were the Unionist equivalent of Quantrill's men: undisciplined and violent guerilla fighters. Despite being mustered into the Confederate army under the Confederate Partisan Ranger Act of August 15, 1862, and rising to the rank of captain, Quantrill was declared an outlaw by Unionist Commander Major General Henry W. Halleck. This had very serious ramifications for Quantrill; if he was captured by the Union, he would be shot rather than being taken prisoner of war. Unfortunately, this proclamation seems to have seriously backfired. Up to this time, Quantrill had behaved as a normal soldier, accepting the principal of enemy surrender. He now moved to a new plateau of instant retaliation, with "no quarter" given to the enemy.

By 1863 Quantrill's Raiders numbered more than four hundred and fifty men, virtually a small army. Bizarrely, the troop also included fifteen-year-old Kate Clarke King, Quantrill's common-law wife, who often dressed as a man and rode with her husband. The Raiders soon escalated their violent anti-Yankee campaign. Quantrill viewed Lawrence, Kansas as a hotbed of pro-Unionist, pro-abolitionists, and a base for Jayhawk raids into Missouri. Another offense in Quantrill's eyes was that the town was also home to Federal Officer James Henry Lane, who had led a brutal attack on Osceola, Missouri and was a leading member of the Kansas Free-Soil campaign. To add fuel to the fire, several women relatives of the Quantrill Raiders had been killed when a prison collapsed in Kansas City. On August 20, 1863, Quantrill assembled his men (who included two infamous pairs of brothers: Frank and Jesse James, and Cole and James Younger) and crossed the border into Kansas. Kidnapping a thirteen-year-old boy, Jacob Rote, from a nearby settlement at Captain's Creek, they forced him to guide them through the moonless night into the town of Lawrence itself.

The Raiders reached the town before sunrise on August 21 and scattered to their pre-arranged positions. The raid was coolly pre-meditated. Weeks before the invasion, Quantrill had sent spies to assess Lawrence's defenses. Thus began one of the worst atrocities of the Civil War. Quantrill's order was "to burn every house and kill every man." Witnesses described the attack as "hell let loose." Men and boys were dragged from their beds and butchered in front of their wives and mothers, even as they begged for their lives and shielded them with their bodies.

Above: Cole Younger also rode with Quantrill and was present at the Lawrence, Kansas, massacre.

Opposite page: The dead Bloody Bill Anderson, shot by Union troops.

From a small-town population of around two thousand, the ruffians murdered one-hundred forty-three men and boys, leaving eighty widows and two-hundred fifty orphans. Few of these people had had any real connection to the Union army. The dead included twenty free African-Americans, including a baby. Many had fled to Lawrence to escape slavery, and two black churches had been founded in the town. Firsthand accounts of the massacre mention black townspeople "being pursued with special malignity." A further twenty-two men and boys were wounded by the gang, and many buildings in the town were torched. As well as robbing and looting the town, Quantrill seems to have invented ethnic cleansing. Perhaps the most appalling aspect of the massacre was that Quantrill himself had lived in the town for over six months (posing as Charles Hart) just a few years earlier, boarding at the City Hotel. It seems very likely that he must have known many of the people that his followers murdered and robbed.

The Confederate leadership was stunned by the brutality of the raid on Lawrence and withdrew their support from Quantrill and his "bushwhacker" gang. Leaders of the Union forces were even more outraged. On August 25, 1863 General Thomas Ewing issued his Order No. 11. This was an eviction notice to anyone who could not prove their loyalty to the Union cause. Its effects were completely devastating. Virtually overnight, the population of Cass County dropped from ten thousand to six hundred.

Unrepentant, just two weeks after the Lawrence Massacre Quantrill and his men were involved in a raid on a Union train in Baxter Springs, Kansas, where ninety-eight soldiers were slaughtered. Much to the embarrassment of the Confederate command, Quantrill continued to lead his men behind Union lines in Texas. But Quantrill's guerilla force soon began to disintegrate into small bands of desperados, some led by Quantrill's "lieutenants:" Bloody Bill Anderson, Frank James, and Archie Clement.

Quantrill was killed by Union forces in May 1865, during a raid in Kentucky. By the end of the following year, Anderson and Clement were also dead.

But even after his death, this "Unreconstructed Rebel" was considered a folk hero by many in Missouri, despite the violence that he and his followers had inflicted on so many civilians. Neither were his tactics forgotten by his followers, many of whom became outlaws and criminals. The James Gang and the Cole brothers went on to apply his methods to bank and train robberies with some success.

The first Quantrill gang reunion took place on May 11, 1888, in the City Hotel in Blue Springs, Missouri. Fourteen former Raiders met at an "ice-cream social" on

the lawn of the hotel to honor Quantrill's mother, Caroline Clarke Quantrill. Mrs. Quantrill was touring the sites of her son's "campaign." According to the *Kansas City Journal*, these ex-guerillas were "an intelligent and well-behaved lot of men, and did not seem possessed of any of the bloodthirsty characteristics ascribed to them. If they ever had, the refining influences of twenty-three years of peace and civilization have evidently transformed them into good law-abiding citizens." These meetings continued until 1929, and were attended by such famous gang members as Frank Gregg and John Noland, an African-American scout who had ridden with Quantrill. The last surviving member of the gang, Frank Smith, died in 1932, at the age of eighty-six.

According to Antonio Mendoza, the author of *Killers on the Loose*, mass murderers are "usually people who aspire to more than they can achieve. They feel excluded from the group they wish to belong to, and develop an irrational, eventually homicidal, hatred of that group. Invariably, they choose to die in an explosion of violence directed at a group they feel oppresses, threatens or excludes them." So what had the poor citizens of Lawrence done to deserve the treatment they received at Quantrill's hands?

Opposite page: Noted guerilla George Maddox, sporting a pair of Remington's 1863 New Model Army pistols.

Remington 1863 New Model Army Revolver

Above: The Remington revolver had a solid frame
which gave the gun good rigidity when firing.

Colt didn't have things all their own way. When Samuel Colt set the price for his Army revolver to the U.S. Government at $25 at the start of the Civil War, he didn't bet on Remington setting the price at just half that for a very competitive weapon. Indeed, in some ways the Remington New Model scored over the Colt. It had a solid frame-making for a more rigid barrel and cylinder under fire. The pistol was based upon a design by Fordyce Beals, and was introduced to the market in 1861. It matched the Colt at a caliber of .44 (designed to suit the Union army) and was a weapon highly valued by soldiers and civilians alike. It was a similar model to the Remington Navy, which was a

.36- caliber weapon. 122,000 examples of the Remington Army revolver were delivered from the company's plants at Ilion and Utica between 1861 and 1875, making it second only to the Colt Army in popularity. This meant that there were many examples still in use on the frontier when the Civil War was over.

George Maddox, "a cold-blooded killer" and member of the Quantrill gang, was famously photographed with a loaded pair of .44 Army revolvers. These were clearly his weapons of choice. A further endorsement by William F. "Buffalo Bill" Cody added enormous kudos to Remington's revolver when he asserted, "It never failed me."

SPECIFICATIONS

Caliber: 0.44

Length of barrel: 8 inches

Barrel shape: Octagonal

Finish: Blue

Grips: Walnut

Action: Single

Year of manufacture: 1863

Manufacturer: Remington Arms Company, Ilion, New York

Below: Detail of the finely machined cylinder and hammer, both of which display a good amount of the original blue steel finish.

Above: The Remington New Model Army Revolver was a major competitor to Colt as the Civil War approached. Its shape, while less elegant than Colt's Army, demonstrated many of the same specifications and proved to be a reliable weapon in action.

Belle Starr

Above: Belle Starr consciously posed as the "Bandit Queen."

Opposite page: Belle Starr poses with Blue Duck, her Native American husband.

"Bandit Queen" Belle Starr was well-known for toting a gun, but preferred to use her intelligence to further her criminal career. She had a life-long association with a cavalcade of famous bad men, including the James brothers and the Youngers, and was wont to use her home as a hideout for criminal gangs, cattle rustlers, and brigands.

Myra Maybelle Shirley was born on her father's farm near Carthage, Missouri, on February 5, 1848. Her father was John Shirley, the black sheep of a well-to-do Virginia family, and her mother was his third wife, Eliza Pennington. By this time the couple was quite prosperous, and raised corn, wheat, hogs, and purebred horses. Belle was one of six children. Her father moved the family into Carthage when the Civil War began and bought an inn, a tavern, a blacksmith's shop, and livery stables in the town. In 1860, his assets were estimated at a considerable $10,000. As the daughter of a well-to-do and cultured family, Belle was educated at the Carthage Female Academy and a private school, Cravens. She was a clever girl, learning Greek, Latin, and Hebrew, as well as playing the piano. But the Shirleys' life took a terrible turn for the worst in 1864 when Union forces burnt Carthage to the ground. Belle's elder brother Bud, who had been a guerilla soldier in the Quantrill Gang, was shot and killed by Union troops in the same year. The family migrated to Scyene in Texas, and it was there that various southern criminals – including the Younger brothers, Jesse James, and various Quantrill members – used their family home as a hideout. It is likely that the Shirley family thought of these men as rebels, fighting some kind of irregular war against the forces of the Union, but it is almost certain that their early influence turned Belle to a life of crime.

Belle married James C. Reed in 1866. Reed was a former Confederate guerilla who had now become a thieving bandit wanted for murder in Arkansas. Their daughter, Rosie Lee ("Pearl") was born in 1868, and their son, James Edwin ("Ed"), was born in 1871. Reed tried to work as a farmer, but became involved with the notorious Starr family (a Cherokee family noted for whiskey-running and stealing cattle and horses), together with the James and Younger gangs. In fact, the couple first lived together at the Indian Territory home of outlaw Tom Starr, just west of

Fort Smith, Arkansas. Jim then moved his young family to Los Angeles, California, trying to avoid his murder charge, but was forced to flee to Texas for passing counterfeit money.

In November 1873, Jim Reed and two accomplices robbed Creek Indian farmer Watt Grayson of $30,000 in gold coins. The family was forced to separate and go into hiding. Belle moved to Dallas, allegedly living off some of the gold from the robbery and operating a livery barn in the town. Belle took to wearing a mannish outfit of buckskins, high-topped boots, a Stetson, and twin holstered pistols. She frequented saloons, drinking and gambling at dice, roulette, and cards. She was also noted for riding through the town while firing her pistols. But she was never glamorous; a contemporary unflatteringly described her as being "bony and flat-chested with a mean mouth; hatchet-faced; gotch-toothed tart."

In 1874 Jim continued with his crime spree, robbing the Austin-San Antonio stagecoach of $2,500. A reward of $7,000 was posted for his capture, and he went into hiding. Belle became a widow when the law finally caught up with Jim near Paris, Texas, on August 6, 1874. He was shot and killed trying to escape.

Forced to earn her own criminal living, Belle left Pearl and Ed with her family and went to live with the Starr family once more. In 1880 she married Samuel Starr. From her new husband's family, Belle learned how to fence goods and animals for rustlers, horse thieves, and bootleggers.

In 1883 Sam and Belle were accused of horse theft by one of their neighbors in Indian Territory, and were brought into Fort Smith to appear before the famous "Hanging" Judge Isaac Parker. Parker sentenced the pair to a year in the Detroit House of Correction. Belle took her punishment, proving herself a model prisoner. But Sam proved much more rebellious and was given hard labor. Both were released in nine months and immediately returned to Indian Territory and their life of crime. In 1886 she was again accused of horse theft, but escaped conviction. But on December 17, 1886 her husband was shot to death by Officer Frank West, who also fell dead in the gunfight.

By now, Belle had taught herself how to manipulate the law and helped acquit several criminals in Judge Parker's court, providing legal advice for Bluford "Blue" Duck (a Cherokee Indian indicted for murder) and her son Ed (charged with horse theft). Blue Duck's sentence of death was commuted to a jail term, while Ed was given a full pardon.

For the final two years of her amoral life, Belle took various lovers, including Blue Duck, Jack Spaniard, Jim Tully, and Jim French. She also married for a third

Opposite page: A studio portrait of Judge Isaac Parker. The "Hanging" judge arrived in Fort Smith in 1875, with a remit to tame the town.

Opposite page: Belle's
equally notorious daughter,
Pearl Starr. Pearl ran a
famous brothel in Fort
Smith.

Below: Blue Duck's Colt
single-action revolver.

time. This time, her husband was a relative of her second husband. Jim July Starr was fifteen years younger than Belle, but their marriage enabled her to live in Indian Territory.

Her irregular and troubled life was brought to an end on February 3, 1889, two days before her forty-first birthday. She was shot in the back while riding home from Eufaula, Oklahoma. Falling from her horse, she was then shot again in the neck and face. There were several suspects, including her husband and son. Ultimately a neighbor, Edgar Watson, was charged with the offense. It was claimed that Belle had threatened to turn him in for a murder he had committed in Florida. But Watson was acquitted of the crime, and it remained unsolved.

Belle's daughter Pearl buried her mother at Younger's Bend on the Canadian River and erected a smart headstone, using her earnings as a prostitute and madam in Fort Smith. It was embellished with various motifs that Pearl felt represented her mother: a bell, a star, and a horse. She also wrote a charming epitaph:

"Shed not for her the bitter tear,
Nor Give the heart to vain regret;
'Tis but the casket that lies here,
The gem that filled it sparkles yet."

Smith & Wesson Schofield Revolver

After the Civil War, the new U.S. Army decided to adopt a standard-issue cartridge revolver, and fixed on the Smith & Wesson Model 3 for their purpose. Lessons learned in the war had shown that cap and ball black powder revolvers were vulnerable, in terms of both slow loading and unreliability in damp conditions. In 1875 the U.S. Ordnance

board granted Smith &Wesson a contract to supply Model 3 revolvers that incorporated improvements to the barrel catch and cartridge ejection, patented by Major George W. Schofield of the U.S. Cavalry. The gun was named after him. The gun was chambered for .45 ammunition, similar to the Colt .45. It had a standard barrel length of seven inches and a blue finish.

Many of the Smith & Wesson Model 3 Schofield revolvers saw service in the Indian Wars and were popular with both lawmen and outlaws in the American West. Reportedly, they were used by Jesse James, John Wesley Hardin, Pat Garrett, Virgil Earp, and Billy the Kid. While the standard barrel length was seven inches, many Schofields were purchased as surplus by distributors who shortened the barrels five inches and refinished them in nickel.

Above: This is the "Second Model" Schofield, which has the circular thumb grip on the barrel latch and no washer behind the retaining pin.

Below: The inspector's cartouche is embossed into the grip. It is still legible.

SPECIFICATIONS

Caliber: .45 S&W

Length of barrel: 7 inches

Barrel shape: Fluted

Finish: Blue steel

Grips: Walnut

Action: Six-round top break single action revolver

Year of manufacture: 1875

Manufacturer: Smith & Wesson, Springfield, Massachusetts

Bill Tilghman

"*He was the man who took a thousand chances, arrested more law gangs, sent more criminals to the penitentiary than any other frontier officer and, with it all, was quiet, soft spoken and gentlemanly.*" – MacLeod Paine

"*The greatest of us all.*" – Bat Masterson speaking about Bill Tilghman.

"*A temperate man who never took a drink.*" – Zoe Tilghman, Bill's second wife.

"*He was the handsomest man I ever met.*" – Marshal E.D. Nix

"*Tilghman would charge Hell with a bucket.*" – Teddy Roosevelt

William Matthew Tilghman Jr.'s career spanned the golden years of the Wild West era and had many of the classic elements of the archetypal gunfighter. He was a dead shot, successful buffalo hunter, saloon owner, rancher, army scout, state senator, and (most essentially) a brave and successful lawman. He was reputed to have earned more reward money than any other law officer in the Old West. But unlike many of the type, Bill was a clean-living, temperate man who believed in the values of fair play and hard work. The March 27, 1898, issue of the *Fort Madison Iowa Chronicle* described him thus: "The officer from Oklahoma is a pleasant gentleman of suave manners, courteous demeanor, and face and eye that show he is not afraid of anything!" Bill was to spend a total of fifty-one years in law enforcement and became the last of the old-time sheriffs.

Bill was born on July 4, 1854, on a hardscrabble farm in Fort Dodge, Iowa, but constant Indian attack forced the family to relocate to Kansas. Like many young men of this era, he grew up as an outdoorsy farm boy, dividing his time between chores, hunting, and fishing. But a chance meeting in the local countryside had a huge impact on the young Bill. Driving the family cart to take his sisters berry-picking, they were approached by a man dressed in buckskins, toting a pair of Colt Navies in his sash, twirling his sleek black mustachios. This impressive dandy was Marshall Bill Hickok. The young Bill Tilghman was thunderstruck, and began to practice target shooting and "drawing" with his father's 1869 Colt Army. Bill's father had been a sharpshooter in the Union army during the Civil War and had been

Left: Bill Tilghman wears a dark shirt and carries a Sharps buffalo gun. He carried his Colt in a reverse-draw flap holster, and wears a cartridge belt. James Elder stands to the right.

partially blinded during his military service. At the age of sixteen, Bill and three of his cousins left the farm to hunt buffalo. Like Bat Masterson, Texas Jack, and thousands of other hopefuls, Bill sought to make his fortune with his "Big Fifty" Sharps. First he joined Bucknam and Rife's buffalo hunting team, then partnered with George Rust to hunt prairie wolves. But in the summer of 1872, and just like the Masterson brothers, Rust and Tilghman won a contract to supply fifty buffalo carcasses a week to the construction workers of the Atchinson, Topeka, and Santa Fe Railroad. Bill was forging a lucrative career on the prairies and persuaded his brother Dick to leave his parents' farm and join him hunting buffalo. But, as was quite common, the hunters were attacked by Native Americans, who were unhappy about the decimation of the buffalo herds. A Cheyenne and Kiowa raiding party launched an attack and killed Dick Tilghman. Devastated, Bill signed on as a cowboy, driving three thousand Longhorn cattle to Wyoming. At the end of the trail, the now twenty-year-old Tilghman decided to ride on to the wild and woolly Dodge City, "the Western Babylon," as it was known. Like many great Westerners before him, Tilghman became a town deputy at $50 a month. But Tilghman found the town too confining, and soon returned to the wide-open prairie spaces. In the winter of 1874, Tilghman hunted with the famous Hurricane Martin around Cimarron, New Mexico, and continued this life for another five years. Over that time, he is reputed to have dispatched over twelve thousand buffalo with his Sharps. But unlike many hunters, who frittered away their earnings on bad women and worse whiskey, by 1875 Bill had saved enough to buy a ranch at Bluff Creek, Kansas. In the same year, he also married a widow by the name of Flora Robinson.

By good fortune, Bill's ranch was next to that of the renowned gunfighter Neal Brown. Like many Western gunfighters, Brown had his own special way of holstering his Colt, in a cross-draw holster concealed in his waistband. The pair successfully worked together on their ranches and in the hide trade. The enterprising Tilghman invested his profits in a Dodge City saloon, the Crystal Palace. It was located next door to the Lone Star Saloon. Henry Garis was his partner in this enterprise. Unfortunately, the proximity of the Lone Star was to prove its undoing. July 4, 1877 was to go down in history as the night when "things blew up at the Lone Star." Groups of cowboys and buffalo hunters entered into a violent brawl. Ultimately, the fracas was subdued by gentleman lawman Bat Masterson. Bill and Henry decided to sell the concern in May 1878. Tilghman reinvested his money in another saloon, the Oasis, which he bought for his brother Frank to run. The local paper joked that the Oasis would serve "Methodist cocktails and hard-shell Baptist lemonade." His

Opposite page: Police Chief Bill Tilghman in later life.

out-of-town business was also in trouble. A Cheyenne war party burned his ranch to the ground. Tilghman and his family rebuilt, but they were wiped out again by the Great Blizzard of 1886. Concerned for his family's safety, Tilghman moved them into Dodge. At around this time, he started working in the law again, as a tracker. He became involved in a New Mexico gunfight in which he shot and killed Arizona Wilson and two of his gang.

In January 1884, Bill was sworn in as a deputy marshal to Marshal Pat Sughrue. Three months later, new Dodge City Mayor George M. Hoover appointed him the town's fully-fledged marshal, with Thomas C. Nixon as his deputy. This was in the post-Dodge City War period, and Tilghman soon became sickened by the political in-fighting between the city's various corrupt factions. He resigned his commission in March 1886. But he was to continue working as a lawman from time to time until the very end of his life. In 1887 he became involved in a notorious gunfight with Ed Prather in Farmer City, Kansas. Drunk and disorderly, Prather started to discharge his gun in the street. Tilghman asked him to take his hand from the gun, but Prather drew instead. Tilghman shot him dead on the spot. Like many other gunmen, Bill evolved a philosophy of gunplay. In his case, he only ever drew his gun (a Colt .38 Special, with a five-and-a-half-inch barrel) if he intended to shoot. When he did shoot, he "aimed at the belt buckle, as that was the broadest target from head to heel." In 1889 he was elected city marshal of Perry, Oklahoma, and was appointed deputy U.S. Marshal in 1892. He moved his family from Dodge City to Chandler, Oklahoma. He also served as sheriff of Lincoln County and was the chief of police in Oklahoma City. At this time, the U.S. government bought two million acres of Indian Territory, with the intention of opening it up to white settlement. As every kind of human poured west, the rule of law was slow to catch up. Bill Tilghman became one of the Three Guardsmen of the Indian Nations, a three-man team of United States Marshals that included Chris Madsen and Heck Thomas. The trio were assembled by U.S. Marshal Evett Nix and worked under his direction. They were also involved with Wyatt Earp, Doc Holiday, Luke Short, and Bat Masterson. These lawmen-gunfighters started to clean up what was to become the state of Oklahoma, arresting or shooting over three-hundred criminals and desperados. These included the outlaw "Cresent" Sam, the Creek Indian Calhoun, and various members of the Doolin Gang ("Wild Bunch"), including Bill Doolin himself as he tried to escape. They also arrested Little Britches and Cattle Annie. The Guardsmen became iconic enforcers of the law, and were said to have even inspired the crimes of men like the Coffey gang, who attempted to rob two Coffeyville, Kansas, banks simultaneously so that they could escape from the Guardsmen's territory.

In 1900, Bill was elected sheriff of Lincoln County, Oklahoma. He also had a model farm in Oakland renowned for its blood stock, Jersey cattle, and Poland hogs. His horse Chant was a Kentucky Derby winner. In 1900, Bill's first wife, Flora, died from tuberculosis after a protracted illness. He remarried three years later, in 1903. His second wife, Zoe Stratton of Ingalls, was twenty-seven years his junior.

In 1904, President Roosevelt appointed Bill a U.S. Marshal and his representative

Opposite page and above: Theodore Roosevelt in 1885. At the time, he was a fledging ranchman. On this page, he poses in his buckskins for a studio portrait, with his gun across his knee.

in Mexico. Roosevelt was hugely impressed by him and asked how "a gunman on the side of the law all of his life was still alive after so many experts had tried to kill him?" Bill replied, "A man who knows he's right has an edge over a man who knows it's wrong!" In fact, it is estimated that Bill had been shot at more than a hundred times in the course of his duties.

His survival skills enabled him to last into the twentieth century, and he became fascinated by the silent movies that were becoming popular. Bill invested some of his money in films about the iconic Western characters he had known and worked with in his colorful career (including the Earp brothers, Doc Holliday, and Bat Masterson). In 1915, he, Nix, and Madsen made the movie *The Passing of the Oklahoma Outlaws*. He also made a second film, *The Bank Robbery*. He interspersed his film work with his work as the chief of police of Oklahoma City.

Tilghman retired in 1910 and was elected to the Oklahoma State Senate. He resigned his seat in 1911, to become head of the Oklahoma City Police Force for a further two-year stint. Retiring once more, Tilghman ran his champion stock ranch from 1913 to 1924. But he obviously missed his time in law enforcement, and in 1924 accepted one final job. He was seventy years of age and had been diagnosed with cancer when he became police chief of Cromwell, Oklahoma. Cromwell was a wild Western town, full of brothels, pool halls, bootlegging, and disreputable saloons. It was known as "the wickedest town in Oklahoma." By this time, Guardsman boss Evett Nix had died from Bright's disease, but the surviving Guardsman Chris Madsen felt that subduing Cromwell would be too much for Tilghman. He warned his slightly younger friend that age had taken its toll, and his draw would have inevitably slowed down.

It was in Ma Murphy's Restaurant in Cromwell that, on Halloween night 1924, a crooked prohibition agent by the name of Wiley Lynn drew a Government 1911 .45 Automatic on Tilghman as Bill tried to arrest him. Although Bill was seventy years old and unwell, the aging gunman still managed to subdue and disarm Lynn, covering him with his Colt .32 Automatic. But for once in his life, Bill broke his cardinal rule and holstered his gun without shooting. Lynn drew a concealed pistol from his pocket and shot Tilghman twice in the chest. Bill was carried to a furniture store next door to the restaurant and bled to death twenty minutes later.

Dave Tutt

Whereas some Western gunfighters were defined by the men they killed, poor Dave Tutt was defined for history by the man who killed him, Wild Bill Hickok.

Davis K. Tutt was born in 1839 in Yellville, Arkansas. His family was involved in the violent Tutt-Everett Feud that was to claim his father's life, so the young Dave became familiar with weapons at a very early age. In 1862, he joined the First Regiment, McBride's Brigade Arkansas (Confederate) Infantry. He served for one year and was then appointed to the quartermaster's department as a wagon master. Once discharged from the army, he made his way to Springfield, Missouri, bringing his mother, sister, and half-brother with him. He made his living at the gambling tables there. This is where he came upon the irascible Bill Hickok, who was also playing in the town. Initially friendly despite having been on different sides in the Civil War (Hickok had fought for the Union), the two men soon fell into a bitter professional rivalry. There were also rumors that Hickok and Tutt had fallen out over women. Tutt

Below: A lithograph of Bill Hickok's shooting of the unfortunate Dave Tutt in the Square at Springfield, Missouri.

believed that Hickok had had an affair with his sister and rejected her, while he had been accused of paying too much attention to Hickok's lover, Susanna Moore. Their relationship went from bad to worse. One night, Hickok became irritated by Tutt's ill humor and refused to play with him. Infuriated, Tutt funded and coached other gamblers to "play" with Hickok, hoping to bankrupt him, but his stooges lost every hand to the far better player.

The adversaries continued to spar in public. One night when Hickok was playing at the Lyon House Hotel in Springfield, Tutt confronted him with a debt of $40 for a horse trade. Hickok paid up, but demurred when Tutt asked him for a further $35, which he said that Hickok owed as a poker debt. Hickok insisted that the debt was only $25, and an argument ensued. Tutt grabbed Hickok's watch off the table, saying that he would keep it as collateral until the debt was settled. The watch was a Waltham

Right: The old Greene County courthouse at Springfield, Missouri, photographed in 1865. Dave Tutt fell and died near the courthouse steps.

Repeater gold pocket watch and was one of Hickok's proudest possessions. Hickok probably wanted to draw on Tutt there and then, but the saloon was full of Dave's friends and allies. Humiliated and angry, Hickok warned Tutt not to wear the watch in public, but Tutt insisted that he would sport the trinket the very next day. Hickok's response to this was unequivocal. "Tutt shouldn't pack that watch across the square

unless dead men can walk." He then collected his winnings and left the hotel.

Seemingly unable to refrain from baiting Hickok, Tutt turned up wearing the watch in the town square the next day, July 21, 1865. In the morning, Tutt and Hickok tried to resolve their differences, but Tutt overplayed his hand, telling Hickok that he now wanted $45 to settle the poker debt. Several other men became

"Wild Bill" James Hickok

involved in the argument, including Eli Armstrong and John Orr. They tried to persuade Tutt to accept $35, but Hickok was adamant that he would only pay Tutt the $25 he had offered the previous evening. At this stage, both men agreed that they didn't want to fight, and went off for a drink together.

But at a few minutes before six that evening, Hickok reappeared in the square, this time brandishing his Colt Navy pistol. He called out to Tutt, who was standing alone in the northwest corner of the square, "Dave, here I am." Hickok holstered his already cocked pistol and called out one final warning to the younger man: "Don't you come across here with that watch." By way of response, Tutt drew his pistol. This was a serious mistake. Although Tutt was renowned as a better marksman, no one could break Hickok's nerve.

Colonel Albert Barnitz, Springfield's military commander, witnessed the gunfight from the balcony of the Lyon House Hotel. He said that both men fired "simultaneously… at the distance of about a hundred paces." Tutt shot wildly, but Hickok steadied his gun on his opposite forearm and took careful aim. Bill's bullet hit Tutt straight in the heart, and the broken gambler collapsed near the courthouse steps. As he fell, Tutt cried out, "Boys, I'm killed."

Two days later, Barnitz arranged for Hickok to be arrested and charged with Tutt's manslaughter. Hickok offered no resistance. Giving evidence, medical examiner Dr. Edwin Ebert reportedly stated that Hickok's bullet "had entered (Tutt's body) on the right side between the fifth and seventh rib and passed out on the left between the fifth and seventh rib." This statement indicates that Tutt was standing side-on to Hickok, in the classic pose of the Western duelist.

Hickok's trial began on August 3, 1865, and lasted three days. The case was prosecuted by Major Robert W. Fyan, and Hickok was represented by Colonel John S. Phelps. Hickok claimed self-defense, and Judge Sempronius Boyd allowed the jury to apply the unwritten law of the "fair fight" to the evidence they heard. Hickok was acquitted, but his local reputation was sullied by the killing.

Ironically, though, it was the publicity around the case that attracted Colonel George Ward Nichols, a writer for *Harper's New Monthly Magazine*, to seek out Hickok. His definitive article about the then-unknown gunman and gambler were to secure Hickok's historical reputation as one of the great legends of the Old West. It was published in February, 1867.

Dave Tutt was buried in the Springfield City Cemetery. But in March 1883, Lewis Tutt, a former slave of the Tutt family, disinterred it and reburied him in the Maple Park Cemetery.

Opposite page: This photograph of Bill Hickok was taken by Wilbur Blakeslee of Mendota, Illinois in 1869. It shows him wearing his guns butts forward for a faster draw.

Colt 1851 Navy Revolver

Above: A detail of the hammer action, frame, and percussion cap "nipples."

SPECIFICATIONS

Caliber: 0.36

Length of barrel: 7 inches

Barrel shape: Octagonal

Finish: Blue steel, brass back strap and trigger guard

Grips: Walnut

Action: Six shot single action repeater

Year of manufacture: 1851-

Manufacturer: Samuel Colt, New York City

The peopling of the West really took off after the Civil War, and the Colt Navy Revolver had been a widely used and popular firearm on both sides of the struggle. Many such weapons were carried west by their owners after leaving military service.

Although widely available, at the time of the frontier the 1851 Navy was to a large extent becoming an obsolete weapon.

Left: One of Colts cleanest and most elegant designs. An all-time classic revolver.

Below: Beautiful glowing walnut grip framed in brass

The gun was loaded with a swivel ramrod, which charged each of the chambers in the cylinder from the front. A percussion cap was then pressed onto each nipple at the rear of the cylinder. This was all quite a performance in an age when rim-fire metal cartridges were becoming the norm and center-fire technology was just around the corner. Because of these limitations, the gun was only able to use relatively low-powered black powder charges. This, coupled with the modest caliber of .36 inches, meant that its stopping power was limited. But it did have the advantage of being a multi-shot weapon when many firearms were still single shot. It was, for example, the gun of choice of Wild Bill Hickok, who carried a pair of these pistols, butt forward to allow for a "twist" or "underhand" style of draw. Despite what we have written about the gun's modest stopping power, in the hands of a skilled gunman, it was still a deadly weapon.

Wild Bill was able to kill his opponent Dave Tutt with a single shot, two hundred feet away across Springfield, Missouri's town square on July 21, 1865. The gun remains a popular collectors' choice, and many people continue to fire the weapons at black powder ranges and at re-enactments.

Gunfighter Filmography

Robert Clay Allison, The "Shootist"

No movies seem to have been made in tribute to the dubious character of Robert Clay Allison, but he does appear in a couple of classic television shows in 1959. First airing on June 15 that year, "Clay Allison" is the ninetieth episode of the long-running series *Tales of Wells Fargo*, which ran from March 1957 to June 1962. Allison is played by Warren Stevens. Clay made a second appearance that year in the sixtieth episode of James Garner's *Maverick* television series, "Full House." In this surreal hour-long episode, Clay Allison appears in company with many other famous westerners (Belle Starr, Cole Younger, and Billy the Kid) as a member of the Bubbly Springs Gang.

Billy The Kid

By contrast, Billy the Kid has been the subject of over fifty different movies, beginning in 1911 with *Billy the Kid*, directed by Laurence Trimble and starring Tefft Johnson. Although many movies inspired by Billy the Kid are of dubious quality (and have put the character in some extremely unlikely situations), there have been some more serious attempts to explore his life and psyche. Several memorable actors have played Billy over the decades. In 1938, Roger Rogers starred in *Billy the Kid Returns*.

Between 1940 and 1943, Peter Stewart, Sherman Scott, and Sam Newfield directed a series of potboiler movies about Billy the Kid. Initially, these featured Bob Steele, who was later replaced by Buster Crabbe.

In 1943, Howard Hughes directed a slightly bizarre study of Billy's life, entitled *The Outlaw*. The film's four main characters are Billy, Doc Holliday, Pat Garrett, and Doc Holliday's girl, Rio McDonald (played by Jane Russell in a succession of revealing outfits). In 1961, Marlon Brando starred in and directed a strange Western adventure called *One-Eyed Jacks*, in which his character, Rio, is heavily based on Billy.

In 1970, Billy featured in the John Wayne movie *Chisum*, where cattle baron John Chisum joins forces with Billy the Kid (played by Geoffrey Devel) to fight the Lincoln County War.

In 1973, classic Western director Sam Peckinpah directed *Pat Garrett and Billy the Kid*, starring James Coburn as Garrett and Kris Kristofferson as Billy.

Young Guns, released in 1988, has been one of the most successful films based on the life of Billy the Kid. Although it does not pretend to document real events,

the movie has a sensible and believable plot. Emilio Estevez plays the part of Billy. A sequel, *Young Guns II,* was released in 1990, also starring Estevez.

Billy the Kid has also become a star of the small screen, with several television credits. In 1989, Gore Vidal's made-for-television movie *Billy the Kid* was shown, starring Val Kilmer. It rejoiced in the tagline, "He was a cold-blooded killer and the all-American boy."

Black Bart

Western director George Sherman directed the below-average *Black Bart, Highwayman,* which was released in 1948. It starred Dan Duryea as the "California stage robber (who) meets European dancer Lola Montez" (played by Yvonne De Carlo). Hardly less amusingly, Black Bart also appears in Mel Brooks' 1974 comedy spoof of Western clichés, *Blazing Saddles*. In Brooks's movie, Bart is a washed-up drunk, locked up in Rock Ridge's town jail, who is then appointed town sheriff. The joke is that he is actually black. Bart was played by Cleavon Little in the movie. In the following year, *Black Bart,* a television spin-off from the movie, was aired. Black Bart is still black, and was played by Louis Gossett Jr.

Butch Cassidy

Butch Cassidy inspired one of the most popular Westerns ever, 1969's *Butch Cassidy and the Sundance Kid*. A winner of four Oscars, the film starred Paul Newman as Butch and Robert Redford as Sundance in one of the most iconic screen pairings of all time. The movie was directed by George Roy Hill. A rather less inspiring film that took Butch Cassidy as its inspiration was released in 2006, Ryan Little's *Outlaw Trail*. Set in 1951, the movie featured Butch Cassidy's fictional grandnephew.

Blackthorn, a kind of sequel to *Butch Cassidy and the Sundance Kid,* is due for release in 2011 or 2012. The movie will feature Sam Shepherd as Butch Cassidy in 1910, as he tries to make it back to America.

The Dalton Gang

The Dalton gang's violent career inspired several movies. The first of these was 1940's *When the Daltons Rode*, which was based on Emmett Dalton's book of the same name. This was followed by *The Dalton Gang* of 1949. Directed by Ford Beebe, the film was a run-of-the-mill Western caper, where two of the Daltons have inexplicably changed their names to Blackie and Guthery. Although Emmett keeps his name, Bob is missing from the film all together. The tagline for the film was "Outlaw Hunt! … For the most daring bad men of a dangerous era…" It sounds like a "B" movie, and it is. "The Dalton Gang", first airing in 1954, was a half-hour episode of the thirty-nine-episode American television series, *Stories of the Century*.

In 1979, the made-for-television movie *The Last Ride of the Dalton Gang* took a light-hearted look at the gang's final raid on Coffeyville, Kansas. Cliff Potts played Bob, Randy Quaid was Grat, Larry Wilcox was cast as Emmett, and Mills Watson played the part of Bill.

The Doolin Gang

The Doolin gang first appeared on the big screen in 1949, in the *Doolins of Oklahoma*. Directed by George Douglas, the film starts as Bill Doolin (Randolph Scott) arrives late at the Coffeyville Massacre, and covers his outlaw career until he is shot to death. The history series *Stories of the Century* devoted its sixteenth episode to the Doolin Gang. The program was first shown in 1954.

Bill Doolin's character reappeared in the 1981 film *Cattle Annie and Little Britches*. By now an ageing outlaw, Bill is played by Scott Glenn.

Wyatt Earp

Without doubt, Wyatt Earp has been one of the best portrayed gunfighters at the movies. He has been played by a wide range of high-caliber movie stars, from Errol Flynn (*Dodge City*) in 1939, to Kevin Costner in his exhaustive 1994 biography, *Wyatt Earp*. In between, Earp has been brought to the big screen by such luminaries as Randolph Scott (*Frontier Marshall* 1939), Henry Fonda (*My Darling Clementine* 1946), Burt Lancaster (*Gunfight at the O.K. Corral* 1957), James Stewart (*Cheyenne Autumn* 1964, this was John Ford's final film), James Garner (*Hour of the Gun* 1967), and Kurt Russell (*Tombstone* 1993), among others. It certainly says something for the magnetic appeal of Earp's legend that so many big stars have wanted to take on the role of this enigmatic lawman. In March 2011, *Variety* reported that Val Kilmer had been cast as Wyatt Earp in a new movie about the legendary gunman, *The First Ride of Wyatt Earp*, to be released sometime in 2012 or 2013.

Robert Ford

Although Bob Ford figures in many movies about Jesse James, he doesn't get many title credits. One exception is the 2007 film, *The Assassination of Jesse James by the*

Coward Robert Ford. In the movie, Ford's motivation for the betrayal of his friend and idol are explored seriously. Directed and written by Andrew Dominick, the film casts Casey Affleck as the tormented Ford.

Pat Garrett

The character of Pat Garrett has appeared in over twenty movies, beginning with *Billy the Kid* of 1930, where he was portrayed by Wallace Beery. Notable portrayals of the venerable lawman include George Montgomery's in the 1958 film, *Badman's Country,* and James Coburn's in *Pat Garrett and Billy the Kid* 1973. This is by far the most well-known movie featuring Pat Garrett. Set in New Mexico in 1881, the movie features an aging Garrett, hired by the local cattlemen to bring down his old friend Billy the Kid. Director Sam Peckinpah cast James Coburn as Garrett, playing against Kris Kristofferson's Billy. Bob Dylan wrote the score for the film, and plays the part of "Alias." The movie's tagline is "Best of enemies. Deadliest of friends." This is a succinct summation of the action.

A completely unconventional view of Garrett is offered in 1988's *Young Guns*, where Patrick Wayne plays a young Garrett in company with younger versions of many other famous westerners. Most recently, the character of Pat Garrett appears in the 2011 movie *The Scarlet Worm*. Played by Michael A. Martinez, the aging gunfighter makes a brief appearance in this very alternative Western.

John Wesley Hardin

John Wesley Hardin has been featured in several movies and television programs. In the 1951 movie *The Texas Rangers,* Hardin was played by John Dehner. More notably, Rock Hudson took the part of Hardin in the 1955 film *The Lawless Breed.* More recently Hardin was played by Max Perlich in the 1994 *Maverick* movie. On television, John Wesley Hardin was one of the subjects in Jim Davis' highly regarded *Stories of the Century* series, where he was played by Richard Webb. In 1959 Hardin was also featured in an episode of the long-running *Maverick*.

He was back on television once more in 1995's mini-series *Streets of Laredo*. Starring James Garner and Sam Shepard, the series was based on a book of the same name by Larry McMurtry. Hardin was played by Randy Quaid.

Wild Bill Hickok

Wild Bill Hickok has been featured in nearly twenty movies, beginning with the

1923 offering, *Wild Bill Hickok,* in which he is played by William S. Hart. More interestingly, Hickok was portrayed by Gary Cooper in Cecil B. DeMille's 1936 movie *The Plainsman* and by Roy Rogers in the 1940 epic *Young Bill Hickok.* Several films about Hickok were released in the 1950s. Most were undistinguished, but Howard Keel's singing Hickok in 1953's *Calamity Jane* is entertaining. In 1977, Charles Bronson played the gunfighter in the surreal movie *The White Buffalo.* Hickok and Crazy Horse team up and roam the plains together, hoping to dispatch this legendary beast. The 1995 film *Wild Bill* is a far more serious portrayal of Hickok at the end of his career. Jeff Bridges' evocation of the aging sheriff of Deadwood shows a man who is worried about his failing eyesight and fully aware that he is likely to end his days violently.

Doc Holliday

Of all the gunfighters of the Old West, Doc Holliday has had one of the most successful posthumous movie careers. Beginning with *Frontier Marshal* in 1939 (where Holliday is played by Cesar Romero), Holliday has appeared in over twenty films and has been portrayed by some of Hollywood's finest actors. These have included Walter Huston in Howard Hughes's 1943 film, *The Outlaw,* Victor Mature in John Ford's 1946 *My Darling Clementine,* Kirk Douglas in *Gunfight at the O.K. Corral* (1957), Val Kilmer in *Tombstone* (1993), and Dennis Quaid in 1994's *Wyatt Earp.* Holliday has also appeared in several iconic television shows. He had his own episode in Jim Davis' *Stories of the Century,* broadcast in 1954, and was played by Dennis Hopper in *Wild Times,* a 1980 mini-series based on Brian Garfield's novel.

Jesse James

Jesse James was even more successful at the movies, featuring in over thirty different films. In the first two movies in which he features, *Jesse James as the Outlaw* and *Jesse James Under the Black Flag,* the part of James was played by his own son, Jesse James Jr. Over the years, James was played by several distinguished actors including Tyrone Power (*Jesse James* 1939), Roy Rogers (*Jesse James at bay* 1941), Robert Duvall (*The Great Northfield Minnesota Raid* 1972), and Kris Kristofferson (*The Last Days of Frank and Jesse James* 1986). There have also been several novelty movies featuring Jesse, including the comedy Western *Alias Jesse James* (1959), where Bob Hope takes the part, and the unlikely-sounding *Jesse James Meets Frankenstein's Daughter* of 1966.

Interest in the notorious bandit has persisted to the present day, and several

Above: Poster for the 2007 movie *The Assassination of Jesse James by the Coward Robert Ford*, directed by Andrew Dominik.

movies featuring James have been made recently. Colin Farrell is Jesse in the 2001 movie, *American Outlaws*, while Brad Pitt takes the role in 2007's *The Assassination of Jesse James by the Coward Robert Ford*. Given the fact that Jesse was actually such an unappealing personality who came to an ignominious end, it seems surprising that big Hollywood stars have always been so eager to tell his story.

Bat Masterson

Of all the Western gunmen, it may be only Bat Masterson and Bill Tilghman that can be seen on film. His figure appears in 1897's boxing documentary, *The Corbett-Fitzsimmons Fight*, complete with his trademark bowler hat. He has been influencing popular culture ever since, and his character has appeared in several movies. In 1943, Masterson was played by Albert Dekker in *The Woman of the Town*, and Randolph Scott in 1947's *Trail Street*. Between 1958 and 1961, Masterson had the distinction of being the inspiration behind a long-running television series, in which he was played by Gene Barry in one hundred and seven episodes. In 1959, Masterson hit the big screen once more in *The Gunfight at Dodge City*, played by Joel McCrae, where he appears during his time as Ford County sheriff. He reappeared more recently in 1994's semi-biographical movie, *Wyatt Earp*, where he is played by Tom Sizemore.

Bizarrely, Bat was also the inspiration behind the Sky Masterson character in the classic musical *Guys And Dolls*. Played by Robert Alda in the original 1950 production, Sky is a high-rolling gambler who is just about to fly to Havana, Cuba. By the end of the show, he is married to the leading lady, Sister Sarah Brown.

Texas Jack Omohundro

A professional showman for much of his life (celebrated in the Hall of Great Western Performers), Texas Jack Omohundro would almost certainly have been delighted to appear in the movies. Two movies featuring Omohundro were made in the early 1930's. *The Adventures of Texas Jack* (1934) was directed by Victor Adamson, and starred Hal Taliaferro as Jack. 1935's *Texas Jack/ Loser's End* starred Jack Perrin in the title role. Texas Jack's character also appeared in Ray Nazarro's 1953 movie *Gun Belt*. Jack was played by Red Morgan. More recently, Texas Jack Vermillion appeared in Kurt Russell's more serious film, *Tombstone* (1993), played by Peter Sherayko.

William Quantrill

William Clarke Quantrill has appeared in several movies about his life, most concentrating on his part in the shocking Lawrence Massacre. In 1940's *Dark Command*, Walter Pidgeon plays a thinly disguised Quantrill (William Cantrell) against John Wayne's sheriff character. In this version of events, Cantrell is killed during the raid on Lawrence. *Kansas Raiders* from 1950 is something similar. Brian Donlevy is Quantrill, and Lawrence is "aflame again." In 1958's *Quantrill's Raiders,* directed by Edward Bernds, Lawrence is depicted in a "shock-hot saga of night-riding terror" and Quantrill is played by Leo Gordon. In *The Young Jesse James* of 1960, "Charlie Quantrill" is shown having a bad influence on the young outlaw. He is played by Emile Meyer. Ang Lee's much more serious, and therefore much more shocking 1999 film, *Ride with the Devil,* shows a brutal portrait of the Civil War South. John Ales makes a brief appearance as Quantrill.

Belle Starr

Although contemporaries described Belle as being a "hatchet-faced; gotch-toothed tart," this was definitely not how she was portrayed by Hollywood. First represented by Betty Compson in the 1928 movie *Court-Martial*, she went on to be played by Gene Tierney (*Belle Starr,* 1941), Isabel Jewell (*Daughter of Belle Starr,* 1946) and, most improbably of all, by the ultra-glamorous Jane Russell (*Montana Belle*, 1952). Later films that feature Belle's character include 1980's *The Long Riders*, where she is played by Pamela Reed.

Belle has also appeared on television, featuring in an episode of the long-running *Stories of the Century* in the early 1950s (played by Marie Windsor), and in series three of *Dr. Quinn, Medicine Woman*, where she appears as a young and vulnerable outlaw.

Right: 1952's *High Noon* contains another famous duel, between Sheriff Will Kane (Gary Cooper) and bad man Frank Miller.

Bill Tilghman

Like many Western lawmen-gunmen, Bill Tilghman had a second career. His was as a movie director and actor. Beginning with the 1908 film, *A Bank Robbery*, Tilghman became fascinated by the storytelling aspects of film making. His first film was only nineteen minutes long, and featured Frank Clanton, Heck Thomas, Quanah Parker, and Tilghman himself, all playing themselves. The movie was made in Cache, Oklahoma. In 1915, Tilghman made a second film, *The Passing of the Oklahoma Outlaws*. This was his attempt to show the dark side of Western life. It starred E.D. Nix, Chris Madsen, and himself, all appearing as themselves.

After his death, Tilghman continued to appear in the movies. In 1981, he was played by Rod Steiger in the 1981 film *Cattle Annie and Little Britches*. Sam Elliott starred as Tilghman in the 1999 made-for-television film *You Know My Name*.

Dave Tutt

Dave Tutt has not received any title billings at the movies, but his fatal shootout with Bill Hickok has had a huge impact on the western genre. From Gary Cooper's *High Noon*, to Clint Eastwood's *Dollars Trilogy*, their iconic duel has been replayed many times. 1995's *Wild Bill* re-enacts the gunfight, with Robert Knott playing the part of Tutt.

Opposite page: 1966's *The Good, the Bad, and the Ugly* was the final movie in Sergio Leone's "Dollars Trilogy." Clint Eastwood often replays the iconic Western duel, as fought by Bill Hickok and Dave Tutt.

Acknowledgements

The Buffalo Bill Historical Center

Kansas State Historical Society

Patrick F. Hogan, Rock Island Auction Company

L.D.S. Church Archives, Museum of Church History and Art, Salt Lake City

National Cowboy Heritage Museum

Mr. Arthur Upham for the Billy the Kid image

J.P. Bell, Fort Smith, Arkansas

Colorado History Society

The National Archives

MPTV, Van Nuys, California

Kathy Weiser, Legends of America